W........
MATTERS
THE SHERPA GUIDE TO
WHAT YOU ARE LOOKING FOR

BRENDA CORBETT AND
JENNIFER CHLOUPEK

WHY IT MATTERS
THE SHERPA GUIDE TO WHAT YOU ARE LOOKING FOR

Brenda Corbett and Jennifer Chloupek

Published and copyright 2014 by
Sasha Corporation - Cincinnati, Ohio USA

Thanks to Contributors:
Karl Corbett
Larry Chloupek
Diane Dew
Bob Welsh
Dr. Justin Kennedy

Printed by Pocket-Pak, The Colony, TX, USA
ww.pocketpak.com

Cover art and layout by Ian McAfee.

Published by Sasha Corporation
Cincinnati, OH, USA

For more information about Sherpa Coaching, their services or products, contact:

Sherpa Coaching   (513) 232-0002
PO Box 417240, Cincinnati, Ohio 45241
info@sherpacoaching.com
www.sherpacoaching.com

Single copy and bulk purchases of this book can be made online at the authors' online store with quantity discounts available.

To order, please visit:
www.sherpacoaching.com/store

DEDICATION

To Karl and Larry: who don't hold back, who live their
Why it Matters and, thank God, share it with us.

CONTENTS

BEGINNING THE CLIMB

POINTS OF THE COMPASS

PERSONAL STORIES

REACHING THE SUMMIT

FOREWORD

Our knowledge and experience provide the foundation for early career success and advancement. To realize our full potential, we also have to reflect on our behavior. The way we conduct ourselves can open doors or limit our opportunities.

Together, our skills and our behavior create an impact on the world around us. We can measure our effectiveness using this equation:

POSITIVE SKILLS PLUS POSITIVE BEHAVIOR CREATE A POSITIVE IMPACT ON BUSINESS

Positive skills plus positive behavior create a positive impact on business (IOB).

The part of the equation most often ignored is behavior. To discover our impact on business, and everything else we do, we can learn the most by looking at our motivators, the engines that drive our behavior.

What drives us? It is easy to talk about situations: "I want to advance my career," or "I'm making a living to provide for my family." External factors are just a small piece of what truly motivates us. More important is our internal source of motivation. Discovering the true source of our motivation requires a journey that very few people know how to take. We have a label for that internal source, our fundamental motivator. We call it Why It Matters.

Your Why It Matters provides the inspiration for what you choose to do, personally and professionally. It is the source of your ultimate sense of personal satisfaction. When you understand the reasons behind your decisions and actions, doors will open, and barriers will fall away.

My own Why It Matters is the common denominator in a lifetime of decision points. I now have a much deeper understanding and appreciation for my true motivation and how it shapes my life.

I have completed my journey of self-discovery. I am delighted that you are about to begin yours.

This book provides stories of Why It Matters, provided by leaders who have discovered their internal mission through the Sherpa Coaching process. Their examples clarify the concept of Why It Matters and illustrate the power of this personal mission statement.

Do not try to guess your Why It Matters. At best, you will come close. It takes guidance and reflection to discover your true source of motivation. I am confident that working with your authors, you will find your Why It Matters. You will harness the strengths associated with that motivation and avoid those moments when it might become a blind spot.

The benefit of your self-discovery will be a great sense of enrichment, accelerated by the learning of others highlighted in this book. Enjoy the journey and your new sense of satisfaction.

STEPHEN M. SUBASIC
Vice President, Human Resources - CDIY
Stanley Black & Decker

PREFACE

My partner, Brenda Corbett, and I have studied human behavior for decades. We have examined the strengths and weaknesses of business leaders around the world. Early in our study, something was missing in our coaching. Learning about strengths and weaknesses helped our clients identify things to work on. It helped them stay focused. It helped them understand themselves better. Still, something was missing.

WHAT WAS MISSING WAS A COMPLETE UNDERSTANDING OF THE REASONS PEOPLE BEHAVE THE WAY THEY DO

What was missing was a complete understanding of the reasons people behave the way they do. We needed deeper insight on individual relationships, business behavior, communication and leadership. We had to get more information about the people we worked with. That is how Why It Matters was born. We knew there was something more. This was it.

One client's story helped solidify the importance of Why It Matters.

Doty told me:

"I am the youngest of three girls. I was treated as the baby. Mom cut up my food and fed it to me. One day when I was five years old, my mom was feeding me a peanut butter and jelly sandwich (all cut up), and my grandmother asked "Why are you still feeding that child? Certainly she can make her own peanut butter and jelly sandwich."

I loved peanut butter and jelly. That day, I started making my own sandwiches. I decided to put as much peanut butter as I possibly could in between those two slices of bread. The more the better I always said. I didn't look back, so much bread and peanut butter and...well, you can guess the rest. I just overdid it. When I was left to do something on my own, I did too much of it. Actually, I overdo everything. No one can ever have a big enough portion. No one can ever have enough of me."

This story brought something important to light. This was not about her strengths. This was not about her weaknesses. It was an important part of who Doty is. That was how the concept of Why It Matters was born. Doty's Why It Matters was "to overdo." That helped her understand all those strengths and weaknesses and give a name to something that has continuously influenced her behavior. Finding those words helped her see an important part of herself.

Finding your Why It Matters takes work. This book breaks it down into four 'compass points' that will clearly give you direction. It will become clear what your Why It Matters is and why you do many of the things you do. This book presents you with an opportunity to reflect. Take your time. Read a page here and a page there. Read a story. Read just one point of the compass, and then put it down.

Finding your Why It Matters is a gift you can give to yourself. When you know this little nugget, you know something that has been hidden deep inside of you.

It requires looking back at your life and recalling significant events that have contributed to the way you think, react, and conduct yourself.

In early 2004, we travelled the country explaining Why It Matters to managers and executives. Understanding our own Why It Matters was a journey in itself. I think I refined my own at least three times. The more you understand the value of getting it right, and using it to build yourself into a stronger, more productive individual, the better off you will be. It is worth it, trust me.

Enjoy the climb. The view at the top is spectacular.

JUDITH COLEMON KINEBREW
Chief Executive Officer
Sherpa Coaching

DEFINITIONS

Don't look any further. In this book you will find what you are looking for. To begin this search, ask yourself: *Why do I do what I do?* The answer to this question will guide your journey to discovery.

As executive coaches, we have studied the matter of motivation. We can help you figure out why you do what you do. The motive, the reason, the thing that drives you has a name: your Why It Matters.

Finding your Why It Matters, finding your deepest motives, will take reflection. Reflection is an organized, chosen activity: looking back on recent events or looking toward the future. We are reflecting when we take stock of ourselves through activities such as keeping a journal. To reflect, you will need to stop for a minute (or longer) and to think through what you do and why you do it. Reflection requires that you step away from noise.

YOUR WHY IT MATTERS REPRESENTS WHAT DRIVES YOU AND CAN BE DISTILLED INTO A PHRASE THAT REPRESENTS YOU.

Finding peace and quiet might require you to spend more time alone. Through reflection, you will stop running, stop doing things, and find some truths about yourself. In the end, your revelations will provide you with a peace that comes from understanding yourself. Your revelations will get you to a better place in your relationships, in your work, and in your life.

To get there we must (must!) reflect. Take time to think about yourself. Reflecting requires an emotional investment. Our biggest obstacle in reflection is the way we use our time. We act on habit, for the most part. We are busy moving forward, doing what we always do. 'Mindfulness' is a term that relates to reflection in neuroscience. It is the technology of reflection. It is the way to become quietly self-aware and notice things. Mindfulness is reflection in the moment. It allows us to become aware of our behaviors (in the split second) before they become self-damaging. That is when you know reflection has worked and changes in behavior have been made.

It's hard, and no one can do it for you. Someone might create a plan for you. They may organize and schedule your activities or analyze a situation for you. However, no one can do your reflection for you. Our heads are filled with planning, organizing, and analyzing. Nothing is wrong with any of those things; they are supposed to put you in control of your life. But if that's all you do, then you aren't really in control no matter how hard you try. In truth, you are reacting, not acting. When you react, you don't always do what's best or make decisions that hold your life together.

Why is it so hard to reflect? Bottom line, we were never taught to. To truly reflect, you have to listen to your own thoughts. Once you listen to your deepest thoughts, you have to do something about them. That can be very difficult because we are just not accustomed to spending our time that way.

So - take a deep breath. Slow down long enough to reflect. Reflect on yourself and your strengths. Keep in mind as we discuss strengths that we are looking at strengths in behavior, not skills. In this context, it doesn't matter whether you can write a marketing plan. That's a skill. It matters that you can get along with people, lead them, and inspire them. That's behavior.

Your journey to discover your Why It Matters can be a steep climb. You will need to be prepared. This book is here to guide you. This book will be your compass. This book will be your Sherpa. Sherpas, the people of Mount Everest, are the guides that bring climbers to the top of that majestic 29,000-foot mountain. They know more about the climb than anyone else. They are the experts.

This climb may take more time and effort than you imagine. You may discover things you were not expecting. To undertake this climb, this adventure, you will need everything a Sherpa has to offer.

We, your authors, are Sherpa coaches. We will help you climb to your own personal summit. Reaching this destination means identifying your Why It Matters. Learning it can benefit everything in your life. By reading this book, you will get in touch with who you are, what moves you, challenges you, and perhaps even haunts you. It will force you to reflect.

REFLECTING IS A CONSCIOUS EXERCISE, A CONVERSATION WITH YOURSELF.

Finding out who you are is an exciting journey. Reflecting is a conscious exercise, a conversation with yourself. You can only do it by taking time to be with YOU. Reflection is the first step in this journey toward finding your Why It Matters.

People are sometimes afraid to reflect. This process will take you to a better place. Trust the process. It is worth the time you take to think about yourself. When you look in the mirror, you will see someone beautiful, someone good-looking, and someone valuable. You will see someone you can understand and appreciate. That person is worthwhile.

Throughout this book, we will share stories to help you connect with the concepts we talk about.

Here is an example of how people can see the same thing in entirely different ways:

A manager wanted to see how his workers felt about their jobs. He went to his building site on the European countryside to take an informal poll.

The manager approached the first worker, Roger, and asked, "What are you doing?"

"What? Are you blind?" Roger snapped. "I'm cutting these boulders with primitive tools and putting them together the way the boss tells me. I'm sweating under this blazing sun, it's back breaking work, and it's boring me to death".

The executive quickly backed away and went off to look for a second worker. He approached Stan. "What are you doing?" he asked. The worker responded, "I'm shaping these boulders into different forms, which are then assembled according to the architect's plan. It's hard work and it sometimes gets repetitive, but I earn a good wage and that supports my family. It's a job. Could be worse."

Somewhat encouraged, he went to a third worker, Milos. "What are you doing?" he asked. "Why, can't you see?" Milos beamed as he lifted his arms to the sky. "I'm building a cathedral! I can imagine the steps over there, filled with throngs of people hurrying inside for a wedding. I can hear the bells ringing out on Sunday morning. I can almost see the way the morning sun will shine through the stained glass, creating beautiful patterns. What a great job."

Three people, all doing the same job, had three very different ways of looking at it.

NAME: ROGER
OCCUPATION: CONSTRUCTION
AGE: 33
WHY IT MATTERS: TO GET THROUGH IT

Roger is single. He has been on the job for two years. Roger focuses on what he is doing . . . breaking stones. He is not happy with his job, and he's not happy with his life. He is just trying to get through the day. Nothing works easily for Roger. He has carried a 'ball and chain' throughout his life.

NAME: STAN
OCCUPATION: CONSTRUCTION
AGE: 51
WHY IT MATTERS: TO PLAN

Stan grew up in the U.S. Stan has planned every minute of his life. When it doesn't turn out the way he plans it, watch out. Stan likes his job. He appreciates his job. It is part of a plan. He makes a living. He is more content than Roger. He is gratified doing it. As long as he continues working his plan, which includes his family and this job, Stan is going to be fine.

NAME: MILOS
OCCUPATION: CONSTRUCTION
AGE: 27
WHY IT MATTERS: TO SEE THE BIG PICTURE

Milos moved from Canada at an early age. Milos has a mission and a vision. His focus on Why It Matters allows him to approach work and life with joy and passion. He looks beyond the task to see the goal. He looks at what the experience will be for the people who come to this cathedral. He is thinking about the fellowship, the weddings that will take place, and the stained glass with the sun shining through it. For Milos, the big picture matters, and Milos is truly inspired.

5

This story serves as a starting point that helps you understand your uniqueness. You truly are 'one of a kind'. We each begin and end our days differently. What happens during the length of our days is based on our Why It Matters. Pursuing Why It Matters makes a statement about who you are.

Here is an absolute truth: this driver, this motivator, can produce uneven results. Sometimes, it will make you happy. Sometimes, it will lead you away from success. Once you discover, understand, and 'own' your Why It Matters, your life will change. When you know what influences you, what drives your decisions, what makes you say the things you say, you will navigate your way toward happiness and toward success.

NAME: BETH
OCCUPATION: DESIGN BUSINESS CEO
AGE: 50
LOCATION: NORTH CAROLINA, USA
WHY IT MATTERS: TO TAKE A RISK

Taking risks can be deeply rooted in some peoples' lives. After discovering her Why It Matters, Beth said her life finally began to make sense. Beth is an entrepreneur. She has started quite a few business ventures. Some failed. Others have flourished. She sees failure as an opportunity to learn and move on.

Reflecting back over her life, Beth saw that 'to take a risk' literally could have cost her life. She got involved in a risky relationship. Before long, she was assaulted and almost killed by her partner. Risk was part of the thrill for her, but this time, it went too far. Now that she knows her Why It Matters, it has fundamentally changed her entire life.

Beth is still a small business owner. She has her share of failures, but she is now aware of what drives her decisions. Beth thinks through to the end of the game before she makes her first move.

Finding Why It Matters was one of the most powerful self-discoveries she has ever made. It might have saved her life.

Concisely, your Why It Matters is the driving force behind what you do. It is at your center, your core. Finding this force means getting to the truth about yourself. Understanding it helps you take full advantage of life. It helps you make good decisions. This discovery can help you regain passion and excitement that has slipped away. It can boost your spirits.

FINDING THIS FORCE MEANS GETTING TO THE TRUTH ABOUT YOURSELF.

You can get closer to your Why It Matters by knowing what you should not look for or expect:

1. Why It Matters is **not** what people say should matter. It only needs to make sense to you.

2. Why It Matters is **not** your purpose or your passion.

3. Why It Matters is **not** a broad metaphysical reason for existence.

4. Why It Matters is **not** a label or category in which to classify the life you have led so far.

Your Why It Matters is not something you do. It is something you are. Our job together is to discover this internal drive, to appreciate where it is flourishing, and to see where it might be holding you back. Discovering your Why It Matters can produce big changes.

We are going to be thinking about the way we learn. There is a word for that: **Metacognition.** Metacognition is an awareness or analysis of one's own learning or thinking processes. It literally means to think about your own thinking. There is a lot of power in knowing how you think. To become someone different, you must pause and reflect on your thoughts before taking action. It takes courage to step outside of yourself and evaluate your behaviors and actions. Metacognition provides you with the opportunity to pause and reflect before taking action. Only then can you make changes.

Metacognitive skills include reflecting on past ways of thinking and making adjustments to your thinking along the way. This might include planning, selecting strategies, analyzing their effectiveness, and making continuous adjustments. Metacognition is a teacher that will guide you and will provide insight to help you learn from past mistakes.

Knowledge alone has no power without action. When you learn about yourself, your next step is to act on what you have discovered. You need to put action behind your thoughts to get the results you desire: new behaviors and better results.

METACOGNITION {REFLECTION}
+ ACTION {DOING}
BEHAVIOR CHANGES {RESULTS}

THE FOUR POINTS

Do you ever slow down long enough to think about why you do the things you do? Truthfully, your life most often runs on autopilot. When you are not required to pay attention, you can become increasingly unaware of why you behave the way you do. Knowing your Why It Matters can be a compass, guiding you to what you are looking for.

This compass will direct your life journey. Your Why It Matters will keep it focused. On this journey to find your personal Why It Matters, you will study the art and science of human behavior.

THIS COMPASS WILL DIRECT YOUR LIFE JOURNEY.

In the last 20 years, knowledge about how we think, the ways in which the brain works, has multiplied exponentially. Experts previously believed that we were creatures totally driven by our biological urges. Then, experts studied how we react to rewards and punishments. This added an extra layer to our understanding. In the workplace, rewards and punishments are now common ways to deal with good and bad behavior.

More recently, scientists have focused on a third drive, internal motivation. This internal motivation, what drives people, can be identified and harnessed. Now, in the workplace, we offer executive coaching to help people figure out what is really important to them and how to be at their best.

Each of us has a summit to climb. As we begin this climb, we refer to this internal motivation as Why It Matters. As we gain altitude, you will better understand what Why It Matters is. You will see it can be used for good. You will come to know that, if this inner motivation is not properly understood, it can also do some real damage.

You are complex. You are also unique. There are over seven billion of us on this planet, all made out of the same chemicals and built on the same framework. We share a common design, almost identical DNA, yet each and every one of us is unique. Each of us has a different experience, and each of us acts uniquely, just like the three builders we talked about earlier. Our uniqueness shows up in the way we communicate and the way we interact with people.

We are undeniably different from each other. We are also different, each one of us, from one day to the next. The cells that make up our physical being change with each breath we take. We grow, we adapt, we react, and we change.

The study of the brain and the nervous system is called neuroscience. This is a rapidly growing body of knowledge that helps explain human behavior. Just as our physical bodies change from day to day, our brains learn, adapt, and react all the time. As we do, our brain physically changes to create and strengthen pathways for our thoughts and feelings. The way we are made affects the way we communicate, achieve results, and respond to demands that face us every day.

Neuroscience tells us that you are not a slave to your emotions. With the right approach, you can choose how you handle situations. You can even choose how emotional you are and where your emotions take you. Changes in your brain truly can be self-directed.

Our friend and colleague, Justin Kennedy, is a professor and researcher of neuroscience based in South Africa. Dr. Kennedy speaks of 'using your brain to change your mind and heal your heart.' This speaks of the power of the human mind. It proves the value you can take from learning about your own thoughts and feelings. Dr. Kennedy is more than an academic working in a laboratory; he is also a Sherpa coach and an integral part of a new movement to marry the discoveries of neuroscience with the practice of executive coaching.

Everybody wants to be happy all the time; at work, at home, everywhere. Executive coaches work on business behavior, guiding leaders and teams to better communication and better relationships. The things executives learn from their coaches apply everywhere in their lives: in their homes, with their families, and out in their communities. They have better personal relationships. Better relationships lead to happiness and satisfaction.

Knowing your Why It Matters will help lead you to happiness. You can choose to become aware, discover your Why It Matters, and be happier in the process. That is a fact.

THIS MOUNTAIN HAS MORE THAN ONE PATH TO THE TOP.

You are heading for the summit. Just as each one of us is unique, each climb will be different. This mountain has more than one path to the top. Even if two people take exactly the same route to the top, there will be slight variations in foot placement, stride length, and a thousand other minute details. Your climb is individual and totally unique to you alone.

To arrive at your Why It Matters, you have to explore four things about yourself. It is helpful to think about a compass as you take this journey. You can remember the four things you have to explore by remembering north, south, east, and west. Each point of the compass will introduce a new way of looking at your Why It Matters.

The points of the compass are each accompanied by a key word that represents part of your life.

- ## NORTH: EXPOSURE
  (your upbringing and experience)
- ## SOUTH: EVIDENCE
  (the basis and foundation for your choices)
- ## WEST: EXCITEMENT
  (you might think of the American Wild West)
- ## EAST: ESSENCE
  (the wisdom of the East, your spiritual side)

Let's look at this in a different way:

- ## NORTH: EXPOSURE
  (stories you have learned from)
- ## SOUTH: EVIDENCE
  (stories you tell to other people)
- ## WEST: EXCITEMENT
  (things that encourage your passion)
- ## EAST: ESSENCE
  (things that give you peace)

We associate these four elements: exposure, evidence, excitement, and essence with points of the compass to make them easier to remember. Let's talk about each one of these briefly before we offer more details.

We begin by exploring the North, **Exposure**. Exposure refers to things you have learned, things you were exposed to as you grew up, from your parents, your school, and your community. We associate exposure with the north. You might remember the television series 'Northern Exposure' as a way to associate 'exposure' and the northern point of the compass. Think of the Aurora Borealis and how vast it is. Think about your experience, and how vast that is. Think about the collection of social, familial, and environmental experiences that have made a mark on your life.

Next is the South: **Evidence**. Evidence refers to the things you tell other people. It represents strengths, weaknesses, stories, and words that form who you are. We associate evidence with the southern point of the compass, the foundation of the world. Evidence is what you say and how you say it. Evidence is the basis upon which people judge you. In our visit to the south, we will look at the way you present yourself to others.

West means **Excitement**: Where do you find your passion? What truly excites you, brings your energy to a higher level? To help us remember, we associate excitement with the western point on the compass. In the 1800s, the western United States was called the Wild West. It was filled with excitement. In our visit to the west, we will explore things in life that make you happy, energized, and fulfilled.

Essence is represented by the East. This is where we find Eastern philosophy. When you look to find what is important to you, you must embrace your relationship with the world. You must come to understand the indispensable qualities that determine your character. This might include your spiritual side and your sense of wonder and mystery.

We will look at EXPOSURE, the stories you have learned from. We will explore EVIDENCE. That's what you tell people about yourself. We will look for EXCITEMENT and ESSENCE and find what is most meaningful in your life.

All together, these elements will help you discover your Why It Matters. Let us look at the four points of your personal compass and continue our climb.

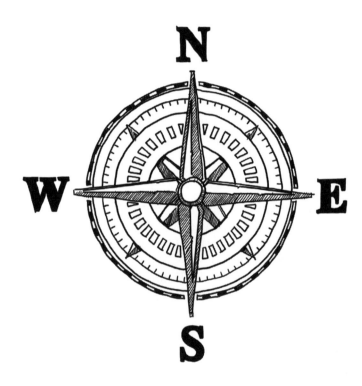

Your Why It Matters is created over time according to a unique recipe. A unique and special set of ingredients has gone into its development. Your Why It Matters is different from anyone else's.

After a while, you might think that our cooks and chefs would run out of ideas and simply be unable to come up with anything new. There are only so many ingredients and a limited number of ways to put them together. However, as you well know, every dish turns out differently, even when cooks and chefs work from the same basic recipe.

Much like a recipe, your Why It Matters consists of a set of ingredients: **Exposure, Evidence, Excitement**, and **Essence**. What happens when life puts those ingredients together? Something unique, something special every time. This guarantees that your Why It Matters is powerfully unique and is worth exploring.

People might choose the same phrase as their Why It Matters, for example, 'to please.' That phrase, 'to please,' means different things to different people. Each person's special combination of Exposure, Evidence, Excitement, and Essence makes them unique.

- For Sophia, 'to please' means saying 'yes' to every opportunity that comes her way.

- Steven has trouble standing up for what he believes, fearing he might offend someone. He works hard 'to please.'

- Miguel is extremely detailed. He wants to make sure his words are clear 'to please' each listener with everything Miguel says.

NAME: MEGAN
OCCUPATION: ACTUARY
AGE: 24
LOCATION: PENNSYLVANIA, USA
WHY IT MATTERS: TO PLEASE

Without any doubt, my Why It Matters is to please. Growing up as the oldest of six children was challenging. I can remember my mother's frustration when each one of us wanted something different, all at the same time. I wanted to help my mother in those situations, so I would do anything she asked me to. I would go along with what my siblings wanted, even though it might have not been something I wanted.

This desire to please served me well in school. I wanted to please my teachers. At times, I could feel frustration and anger well up inside me when they were unhappy with me. I would often take solitude in my room, releasing the frustration and anger with tears. Hidden in my room, no one knew what was going on.

This followed me to my adult life. Pleasing people has worked for me in some situations, but most recently this desire to please has robbed me of my own voice. I don't offer opinions. I am 'stuck' professionally. Now, things have changed. I am weighing the costs and benefits of pleasing others when I can't please myself. It is a journey, but a journey I am excited to begin.

Why It Matters. We describe it in a few words, but it is not always simple. It's deep. It's different. Even if someone else uses the same phrase to describe Why It Matters, yours is personal. As you discover your Why It Matters, this will become clear.

NORTH: EXPOSURE

We associate north on the compass with the word 'exposure.' What have you been exposed to? What has the world taught you? One way to help find your Why It Matters is to review your past. Let's look at your family and social experiences. This is an opportunity to review the ways in which your past has influenced the person you are today.

When you look at the northern sky, you see the Northern Lights. You see the North Star. You see much of the history of our universe in the night skies. Now, let's look at your history and the story of your life.

YOUR WHY IT MATTERS IS INGRAINED IN YOUR PERSONALITY.

Your Why It Matters is created by Exposure:

Your Why It Matters is part of who you are. It has been with you for many years. Your Why It Matters is ingrained in your personality. Your upbringing will shed light on why you do the things you do today. Looking at your history and your experiences will help you identify your Why It Matters.

Let's look at your **Exposure**:

It is divided into **People**, **Places**, and **Things**. With the knowledge from your people, places, and things in the past, you have created and developed your values.

PEOPLE

Stop and think about yourself growing up. Someone got you dressed, fed you, got you ready for school, and prepared you for life. Whoever it was, that person affected your thought process and your actions. As your parents took care of you, certain things happened consistently. Certain things were said regularly. Your parents often handled things the same way. The behavior they displayed can help you discover your Why It Matters.

Messages you heard growing up:
* *What has your mother or father said since you were a child?*
* *What did they say was important and vital for a good life?*
* *What did they say that might not have been important, but was said quite often?*
* *As you were walking out of the house, going to school, what did they say?*
* *As you graduated from high school, what was their advice?*

NAME: ABBY
OCCUPATION: PHD
AGE: 25
LOCATION: NEW YORK, USA
WHY IT MATTERS: TO BE ACKNOWLEDGED

Abby spent a lot of her childhood looking for recognition. She was criticized every time she walked into her home. As a teenager, Abby twirled her hair with her forefinger all the time. During dinner and during conversation, she would play with her hair. She will tell you that she did it because her mom always said something about it. Every time she played with her hair, she got attention from her mother. There were not many other ways in which she could guarantee attention from her mother.

Abby's Why It Matters is to be acknowledged. In every situation, if Abby is acknowledged, she is in great shape and can conquer the world. If she is ignored, or feels as if she is being ignored, she will show her weaknesses, and become flustered.

Do you have children? If so, think about what you say to your children. Just as your parents did, you are constantly sending messages to your children. Those messages are based on all your experiences in your life. Imagine your kids are heading out to school to start a new year, or asking for advice about something important. What do you say to them? The words you heard from your parents, and the words you say to your children can help you discover your Why It Matters.

- *What do you tell your children?*
- *What is important for them to know in life?*
- *What do they need to be successful?*
- *What do you tell them daily? Often?*
- *When something goes wrong with your kids, what do you say?*

Andrew is a busy finance director for a Fortune 500 company. He is excellent at his job and a true perfectionist in his conduct at work. He has three children, all younger than 10 years old. He is in charge of waking up his kids in the morning. This is what he says to them every single day: 'Emily, Jason, Erik . . . tell me three things you are going to do correctly today.'

Andrew's Why It Matters is clear and consistent through his messages to his children. He makes sure his kids hear it every day.

Your parents and caretakers had a deep and profound impact on your Why It Matters. They were not the only ones. Think about the other people in your life. What about the building blocks of your character that were created by your guides, your coaches, your teachers, and people you looked up to? What about mentors? Who has had a lasting effect on your life? What did they teach you?

PLACES AND THINGS

The places you 'hung out' during your upbringing are part of this exposure package.

- *How did your environment shape you? Think about school, church, and extended family.*
- *What did you get from hobbies, sports, and activities?*
- *What lessons from your environment have you brought into your life today?*

Put all of these past experiences together, and you get the things you grew up with. The accumulation of all the things that have happened will help you know for a fact what your Why It Matters is. This is your proof. In your identification of your Why It Matters, the things you have been exposed to will reflect what you call your Why It Matters.

VALUES

Exposure examines what you have been subjected to in life: your upbringing and your experiences with people who have influenced you. All of that is reflected in your standards, in your principles, in the ways things take on special importance to you. We call these things values.

Picture yourself climbing a mountain, heading toward your personal summit. The base of this mountain is made up of your personal values. Let's begin our climb by identifying the values you live by. Make them clear and memorable, so you can remember them and share them with others.

Values are the principles and standards that are intrinsic to you and the way you behave. When you act, communicate, or respond the way you do, your values are on display.

Your values matter because, ultimately, they guide your behavior. Your values are part of the fuel that pushes your Why It Matters. Identifying your values will get you one step closer to identifying your Why It Matters.

If your number one value is family and you are asked to work an additional ten hours this week to complete a deadline, how do you respond? What is your thought process? How do you balance your family with your job? The way you act and feel in this situation and the way you respond to this request clearly shows your values to the world.

The way you live your life displays your values. You can't say you place great value on something because you like the sound of it or because you think you should place value on it. Your values must represent truth in your life.

VALUES

Pick the values that you believe to be very important in your life.
Then, write the **three** most important ones on the lines next to the list.

TOP 3 VALUES:

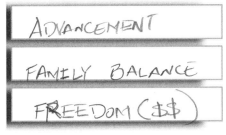

ADVANCEMENT

FAMILY BALANCE

FREEDOM ($$)

Transfer these values to page 66 to have your story all on one page.

- **Accomplishment**
  (a sense of mastery and achievement)
- **Advancement**
  (progress up a ladder)
- **Adventure**
  (new and challenging experiences)
- **Competitiveness**
  (winning, taking risks)
- **Cooperation**
  (teamwork, getting along)
- **Creativity**
  (imaginative, innovative)
- **Economic security**
  (steady, adequate income)
- **Family Balance**
  (family members are satisfied)
- **Freedom**
  (independence, autonomy)
- **Friendship**
  (close relationships with others)
- **Health**
  (physical and mental well-being)
- **Honesty**
  (truth)
- **Inner Harmony**
  (at peace with oneself)
- **Integrity**
  (sincerity, standing up for beliefs)
- **Involvement**
  (belonging, participating)
- **Loyalty**
  (duty, respectfulness, obedience)
- **Pleasure**
  (fun, laughter, comfort)

WHY IT MATTERS: YOUR EXPOSURE

What were your messages and motivators from:

People:

UNCLE; MOTHER & FRIEND'S PARENTS

Places:

· VISITS AND CAMPING TRIPS
- TENNIS CLUBS
- NEIGHBORHOOD

Things:

- PROGRESS IN THEIR LIVES - HOMES, CAREERS, SUMMER VACATIONS
- SENSE OF FINANCIAL SECURITY

Where do you see them in your life today?

- I FEEL LIKE (AT LEAST I AM TOLD) I HAVE DONE WELL. I HAVE ACHIEVED MORE THAN THEM.
- I STILL LOOKUP TO THEM; I SHOULD/COULD DO BETTER

What were you taught by your experiences that supports your values?

- I HAVE TO WORK HARD (ER) EVER YEAR
- IT'S A JOURNEY
- NEVER SETTLE FOR WHAT I HAVE
- TAKE CARE OF MY FAMILY (MOST IMPORTATLY, MAKE THEM PROUD)

24

SOUTH: EVIDENCE

By identifying your values in the **Exposure** phase, you have already begun to collect solid information. Values are a good starting place to help you begin your identification of strengths and weaknesses. Keep your list of values handy while we dig a little deeper.

Let's go south, the next point on the compass, and build upon what we know. The key word here is **Evidence:**

We will examine personal evidence:
- **Your strengths**
- **Your weaknesses**
- **Words you say**
- **Stories you share**

That will get us closer to the discovery of your Why It Matters.

Think of the South Pole. It's the bottom of the world. Think of the south as the base, the foundation of the world. Your Evidence is the foundation and basis upon which people assess you. The evidence we are looking for will help to show us the basis of your choices, decisions, attitudes, behaviors, and opinions. While collecting your personal evidence, you need to be both subject and the scientist in your own Why It Matters experiment. Your mission is to record your strengths, weaknesses, words, and stories.

Your Why It Matters is built into each and every one of your stories. Once you start consciously listening and recording what you say, you begin to see your driving force. It is rather fascinating.

Once you do this for yourself, then finding other people's Why It Matters will become a pastime. You will gain a great deal from knowing Why It Matters for important people in your life.

To examine your strengths and weaknesses and look into your words and stories, you have to stop for a second. You have to reflect. You have to breathe. We have to examine the art of reflecting because to tell you the truth, people usually don't reflect. They just go, go, go and don't stop to think about life. Reflection involves a search for meaning, purpose, and truth. It's important.

STRENGTHS:

How many times have you received a compliment regarding something that you did? Has anyone ever told you:

- *You are so creative!*
- *Wow, you're a brilliant problem solver!*
- *You have a way of bringing people together.*
- *You get the job done.*

All of those are nice compliments. More importantly, they are related to your strengths, areas in which you can provide consistently high performance. Maybe you already knew they were your strengths, or maybe it was the first time you received a compliment on the topic.

There are two ways to catalog your strengths. First, there are strengths that are already known to you. You use them to your full advantage. Second, there are strengths you possess that you do not know about yet.

Let's identify both kinds of strengths: the **known** and the **unknown**.

You can say that a 'known' strength is something 'in your wheelhouse.' The term wheelhouse refers to a position of strength and safety or to a situation that allows you to produce maximum results. Your wheelhouse is an area of expertise specific to you. It refers to things that come naturally for you. Your strengths are centered on things you do well. When you are exhibiting your strengths, you are in your comfort zone. You can handle the situation in front of you with ease because you know you are good at it.

Think about a time when you were deeply involved in a meaningful project and time just disappeared. Everything worked. People got along. The project was flawless. Your strengths, the way you handled yourself resulted in excellence. Strength most often occurs automatically without you thinking much about your actions. Strengths are your 'comfort zone' behaviors.

NAME: JOHN
OCCUPATION: HOSPITAL ADMINISTRATOR
AGE: 43
LOCATION: WISCONSIN, USA
WHY IT MATTERS: TO CONTEMPLATE

John describes how he solves a problem in this way:
"I hear a problem from one of my direct reports. I ask them to describe the problem again using a different point of view. Then I ask them to come back at the end of the day to discuss the solutions. When the direct report leaves, I sit back in my chair. I think through three different ways of handling the problem. This is very effective. At the end of the day, I always have at least one solution that is the same as my direct report's. Taking time works for them and for me. We end up on the same page."

Looking at strengths, we see that John takes time with decisions and doesn't rush his direct reports. He clearly cares about his people and their problems.

Look at the situations below. Your immediate answer is likely to be a known strength. **Write the number in the box.**

When a problem arises, do you:

1. *Take your time, analyze the data, and then make the decision.*
2. *Dive in head first, make the decision, and go with it.*
3. *Ask your colleagues, peers, friends, etc. for their opinion.*
4. *Other:* _____

What do you do in a social situation?

1. *Immediately go and meet new people.*
2. *Stand back and observe the situation.*
3. *Seek out familiar faces.*
4. *Other:* _____

How do you set goals?

1. *I have weekly, monthly, and yearly goals.*
2. *I can navigate through life without planning.*
3. *End results ~~are all that~~ matters* THE MOST.
4. *Other:* _____

You have quick answers for these questions.
Your immediate answer is in your comfort zone.

Have you ever thought about what makes you drawn to certain activities over others?

When given the option to create your day, what tasks will you tackle?

Being uniquely made, we all have specific strengths that set us apart. We are naturally drawn to activities that highlight our strengths. It is easier to get into a comfort zone when you are using your strengths.

Answers to these questions help identify your known strengths.

- *What is my comfort zone?*
- *What strengths do I use in the zone?*
- *What happens when I perform tasks in the zone?*
- *How do I choose to spend my energy and time?*
- *In what areas am I a 'natural' at doing things?*
- *What have I learned recently that I love doing?*
- *What keeps me going all day?*

Write your known strengths below:

- DECISION MAKING; CHANGE MANAGEMENT
GETTING THINGS DONE; CONNECTING W/ PEOPLE
CREATING NEW RELATIONSHIP; SPENDING TIME
WITH FAMILY AND FRIENDS

Now that you have your known strengths, it is time to see whether you have strengths you are not aware of: unknown strengths. You will do this by collecting feedback from others. Asking for feedback will give you the opportunity for someone else to hold up a mirror to help you see your strengths.

Ask three people closest to you what your three strengths are, or ask them to provide you with a brief story of when you were at your best. Don't corner them. Give them time to think about it. One of the best ways to ask is to send them an email.

For example:

Dear Mary,

I am taking a hard look at myself and would like your opinion about me. What do you see as my three biggest strengths? I really appreciate you answering this question.

OR

Can you remember a time when I was performing at my best? Can you please email me the story that best captures that scenario? What did I do?

You might receive feedback validating your already known "wheelhouse" strengths, or you might receive feedback regarding strengths you were totally unaware of.

Write what you have learned about your strengths:

_____

_____

_____

Sometimes it helps to see lists. Here is a list of 30 common strengths. **Circle the three you think describe you, or add your own below:**

Enthusiastic — Direct — Attentive — Outgoing

Decisive — Dedicated — Inclusive — Centered

Tenacious — Humble — Responsible — Patient

Persistent — Passionate — Trustworthy — Generous

Optimistic — Open — Organized — Approachable

Accurate — Driven — Honest — Passionate

Reliable — Cheerful — Relaxed — Thoughtful

Observant — Conscientious

This will give you a great place to start when you are looking for your Why It Matters. **Celebrate your strengths.** They are what got you where you are today. You are something special.

WEAKNESSES

Let's continue to look at **Evidence**. We have examined your strengths. Now let's visit your weaknesses. To successfully identify your Why It Matters, you must learn about your weaknesses and how to address them. They can be the biggest clue in the discovery of your Why It Matters.

Keep in mind that as we discuss weaknesses, we are considering behavior, not skills. Are you dreadful with financial statements? In this context, it doesn't matter. That's a skill. Do you sometimes fail to get your message across or leave people uninspired? That's behavior. That is what we are working with.

If you walk into a bookstore or search online, you will see countless books on how to identify your strengths. You will be hard pressed to find books that teach you how to identify your weaknesses. Conduct an online search for "how to identify your strengths." Then do a search on "how to identify your weaknesses." Strengths win out by a three to one margin or more. Strengths are easier to talk about.

LEARN TO EMBRACE YOUR WEAKNESSES.

People in every culture find it difficult to speak frankly about weaknesses. Weaknesses are human. We all have them, so why are we hesitant in identifying them? Learn to embrace your weaknesses.

Your strengths got you to where you are today. Your weaknesses are holding you back. Your weaknesses keep you from reaching higher ground. You have to identify and take responsibility for your weaknesses. **You have to face your weaknesses in order to reach your summit.**

Weaknesses are not crimes or failures. They are simply something to be aware of. Once these behaviors are identified, you can move from where you were to where you ought to be. Sometimes, your weaknesses are right in front of you.

NAME: MAUREEN
OCCUPATION: CEO
AGE: 44
LOCATION: LOUISIANA, USA
WHY IT MATTERS: TO BE TENACIOUS

Maureen is a passionate woman at work. She cares about her job. Passion is often a good thing, but it can work against you.

When she gets emotional, she will say things like, 'You are not pulling your weight on this task,' or 'He is not trying hard enough.' She is so passionate about getting things done that people don't think she cares about them personally. She will say things that cost her respect and the appreciation of the people around her.

Maureen's Why It Matters is "to be tenacious." She never gives up. She stays with things all the way to the end. Maureen is driven to be tenacious in everything she does. Usually this turns out all right. When she appears to care more about the work than the people, this driver becomes a problem. So when her tenacity plays out negatively and she loses the respect of the people around her, it is definitely a weakness. She continues to be more aware of this when it happens.

Your weaknesses don't define you. Work on them, and they will refine you.

We have talked about reflecting. It is that time again. This might be uncomfortable at first, but stay with it. Begin to reflect on the following areas. Let's discover what might be holding you back from being at your best.

Can you see a weakness that might be holding you back in your…
- *Personal life?*
- *Professional life?*
- *Social life?*
- *Spiritual life?*

There are two ways to catalog your weaknesses. First, there are weaknesses that are already known to you. You try to work around them or overcome them. Second, you have weaknesses that you are not aware of yet.

Let's look at the known weaknesses. You have examined your strengths. If you fall back on your strengths without conscious choice, you can rely on your strengths too often. Overused strengths can be weaknesses. By going back and revisiting your strengths, you might already begin to see a connection. When you list your strengths, think about what that strength might look like when it is overused. When you have identified your strengths, your weakness can easily fall into place.

Let's go back to a story we heard in examining 'strengths' and dig a little deeper.

NAME: JOHN
OCCUPATION: HOSPITAL ADMINISTRATOR
AGE: 43
LOCATION: WISCONSIN, USA
WHY IT MATTERS: TO CONTEMPLATE

John told us, "I hear a problem from one of my direct reports. I ask them to describe the problem again, using a different point of view. Then I ask them to come back at the end of the day to discuss the solutions. When the direct report leaves I sit back in my chair. I think through three different ways of handling the problem. At the end of the day, I always have at least one solution that is the same as my direct report's. Taking time works for them and for me."

Can this be a weakness? When John sits back in his comfortable chair, he might take too long to deal with a minor issue. Perhaps his attention should be on something more important, something that only he can deal with. There is a distressing flaw in John's behavior, too: When an employee brings John a problem, he takes ownership of it. He enjoys reflecting on minor issues. He ends up solving everything for his people. This could end up being a critical weakness.

Here are some examples of strengths that become weaknesses through overuse:

STRENGTH   WEAKNESS

STRENGTH		WEAKNESS
Enthusiastic	⟶	*Intimidating*
Decisive	⟶	*Argumentative*
Tenacious	⟶	*Inflexible*
Persistent	⟶	*Annoying*
Optimistic	⟶	*Insincere*
Agreeable	⟶	*Non-confrontational*
Direct	⟶	*Rude*
Humble	⟶	*Manipulative*
Results focused	⟶	*Tunnel vision*

Here is one example: Perhaps your strength is in being direct. You don't wait for people to figure things out. You tell them because you already know. Your strength, when it is overused, might appear to be impatience.

Is impatience a weakness?
Let's ask a few questions:

- *What does your impatience look like at work?*
- *What does impatience look like at home, with family and friends?*
- *What is the cost of being impatient?*

Take a minute. Come up with real answers specific to you.

Let's revisit your strengths. **Please write them below, and then look at them from a different perspective.**

What do your strengths look like when they are overused?

STRENGTH   OVERUSE

Well, now let's find the weaknesses you are not aware of. Feedback is the process of receiving information from another person. Sometimes hearing about your shortcomings is awkward and even painful. You are going to ask trusted friends and colleagues for honest feedback.

As you request feedback about your weaknesses, focus on what you are asking for. You want sincere, honest, and open responses. That means you have to be sincere, honest, and open in asking for answers.

Asking can be difficult, but the results will get you to a better place. It is critical that you know who you are in other people's eyes. You have to be ready for the truth. You have to be prepared to listen without making any comments.

You may have to prepare the person you are asking. They have never been asked to participate in this kind of conversation. Give them time. Let them feel that you really want the answer. Do not comment on their response.

Here's how that dialog might go:

NAME: MATHIEU
OCCUPATION: PHARMACIST
AGE: 40
LOCATION: QUEBEC, CANADA
WHY IT MATTERS: TO GET IT DONE

Mathieu works really, really hard. He is a doer. Mathieu doesn't have a lot of time for people that slack off or take longer than he wants to get something done. He asked his three direct reports what his weaknesses were.

Mathieu: *So, I am in the middle of a very personal experience. I am being coached, and it is really helping me connect to my weaknesses. What I do well, and what I don't do well. Can you help me?*
Frank: *Yeah, I guess.*
Mathieu: *I want to know what you think I need to work on to be a more effective boss.*
Frank: *Are you serious?*
Mathieu: *Yeah, dead serious. And I really would appreciate your opinion…. the truth.*
Frank: *Well, here's the thing. I don't think you really care about me.*
Mathieu: *What makes you say that?*
Frank: *I am not as fast as you are. I am new in this business, but you just don't seem to care about that. I would appreciate if you gave me some slack, let me do things in my own time.*
Mathieu: *Thank you Frank, I really didn't realize you felt that way. I will work on it.*

Feedback questions to examine your weaknesses:

- *What do you consider my strengths?*
- *What does it look like when I overuse these strengths?*
- *What are my blind spots?*
- *Who are some people I should emulate?*
- *What would that look like?*
- *What could I be doing more of as a manager?*
- *What should I stop doing?*
- *Where do you see my biggest room for improvement?*

NAME: ALLISON
OCCUPATION: PROGRAM MANAGER
AGE: 29
LOCATION: DISTRICT OF COLUMBIA, USA
WHY IT MATTERS: TO ACHIEVE

I love to get things done. I am really versatile, so I can work on my own. I can focus intensely for long periods of time. It's my strength: intense focus.

I had no idea that one of my weaknesses was body language. I asked a trusted colleague to help me identify my weaknesses; I thought my facial expressions were fine. I was totally unaware that when subordinates walk by my office they think I am mad because of the way I look.

When I am extremely focused on something, I have an unintended scowl on my face, and my eyebrows are raised and moved inward. I learned to pause periodically, consciously doing facial exercises. I learned to glance up, and say "Hi!" when folks walk by my office.

You fix the weaknesses by becoming aware of them. Once you are aware of them, you have to observe when they happen. You have to see when, where, who they happen with.

Here is a list of weaknesses people have identified in their behavior. Maybe these can help you refine your list:

Intimidating	Rude	Shy	Lazy
Noninclusive	Prejudiced	Ignorant	Sloppy
Stubborn	Manipulative	Aggressive	Impatient
Annoying	Overbearing	Judgmental	Intolerant
Gossiping	Insincere	Talkative	Moody
Insecure	Inflexible	Obsessive	Rigid

Let's capture your thoughts as you reflect on weaknesses. Based on my own analysis and feedback from others, here are three shortfalls in my behavior.

These are my weaknesses:

_____

_____

Now that you have discovered your weaknesses, it is time for a celebration. Knowing your weaknesses brings you one step closer to discovering your Why It Matters. Another reason to celebrate: now that you have identified your weaknesses, you can begin to identify replacement behaviors that will work for you and make life just a little easier.

Here's where this gets interesting. Identifying weaknesses is one of the biggest clues you will uncover in your search for Why It Matters. Quite often, you will see that a weakness in behavior is your Why It Matters run amok.

Running amok. The term applies to something that has gone wild, gone out of control, gone badly.

How does your weakness relate to your Why It Matters?

Your weakness shows up because you are unable to satisfy, fulfill, or realize your Why It Matters. Your weakness appears because your Why It Matters has been thwarted or threatened. Working backwards, if you notice when a weakness appears, you then can figure out what part of you has been challenged. Once you figure where the threat is, you can then identify your Why It Matters. Examples:

WHY IT MATTERS – TO GET IT DONE.
Someone or something slows you down. When you can't get up to speed and be the fastest person on your team, you react with frustration (a weakness). You are seeing Why It Matters run amok.

WHY IT MATTERS – TO ACCOMMODATE.
If you can't accommodate people, for whatever reason, you feel as if you have failed. You are unhappy and uncomfortable in their presence. You shut down and don't talk to anyone (a weakness). This is your Why It Matters run amok.

WHY IT MATTERS – TO BE THE EXPERT.
You want to stand out, to be regarded as the best, the most sophisticated. You rehearse a presentation. Your boss says, "Your presentation stinks. You have to redo it." You react by taking it personally. You get angry. Without meaning to, you insult your boss (a weakness). This is your Why It Matters run amok.

Let's move on to more **Evidence**. We have searched strengths and weaknesses. Now, let us look at the words you say, the stories you share. Words and Stories. Think about it.

WORDS AND STORIES

Words build meaning. Your words reveal what you think is meaningful. Often, your words are assigned great value. Think about words for a minute. We don't spend enough time reflecting on words; the power of the words you say, the power of the words you use in any given circumstance. Spend a day (tomorrow), and hear the words, think about the definition, and reflect on how the words have been heard.

WE DON'T SPEND ENOUGH TIME REFLECTING ON WORDS.

If you hear the word 'family,' what do you think of? How do you define 'family'? Ask five people their definition, and you will get five different interpretations. None of them are incorrect.

What about 'home'? 'Integrity'? Same thing, different definitions from each person.

If you look these words up, you will find multiple definitions. The definitions that 'ring true' for you will depend on your **Exposure**. Your words and their definitions are yours alone. The impact of your words and the stories you share are profound. Don't take words lightly, as they can easily leave a mark. **What do you say? What are your 'go to' words?**

NAME: ALBERTO
OCCUPATION: MUSICIAN
AGE: 54
LOCATION: MADRID, SPAIN
WHY IT MATTERS: TO BE RESPECTED

Alberto is married to a woman named Estella. They work together, with Estella handling business matters for Alberto's band. Estella takes a long time to get ready to go out. If she and Alberto are expected at a meeting, she often runs late. Alberto often says to her, 'You don't respect me. How can you be late? You must really not respect me.'

Clearly, there is no direct link between tardiness and respect. Frankly, Estella is just disorganized. The use of the word 'respect' says more about Alberto than it says about Estella. In fact, the words he uses provide evidence to Alberto's Why It Matters.

Your Why It Matters is found by looking at words. Your words. Words that describe you. Words you use to describe the world. Words that speak to your thoughts and principles. Words you use consistently with people you care about. All of these words are a reflection of your Why It Matters.

NAME: BUD
OCCUPATION: VICE PRESIDENT OF SALES
AGE: 60
LOCATION: MARYLAND, USA
WHY IT MATTERS: TO BE VALUABLE

Bud is the top sales representative for a large pharmaceutical firm. Bud enjoys spending time with clients sharing a meal in a casual atmosphere; Bud often tells stories from his past and about his favorite customers. On a regular basis, he talks about a customer who considered him the most valuable salesman he ever met. Have dinner with Bud a second time, and you are likely to hear the same story again.

This and others of Bud's stories have a common denominator: how valuable Bud is to the company and to his clients. His stories reflect his Why It Matters.

Ask Yourself:
What stories do I like to tell?
Is there a theme to these stories?
What are my five most commonly used words?
What do I say/repeat to those I love?

S

SUMMARY

So you have all the **Evidence** you need to find your Why It Matters. You know your strengths. You have identified your weaknesses. You know the words you use most often. You know the stories you repeat.

WHY IT MATTERS: YOUR EVIDENCE

Complete the form below, and then transfer to page 66 to have your story all on one page.

What are your strengths?

What are your weaknesses?

What are your words?

What are your stories?

WEST: EXCITEMENT

Let's look to the west, and look for the **Excitement** in your life. No matter where you live in the world, you have heard about America's Wild West. Cowboys, gunfights, wild horses, exploring the land and discovering gold. All of these words bring up some sort of excitement, for men and women, young and old alike. Even though it all happened many, many years ago, there is just a little thrill in all of us, thinking about that period in history.

That excitement, that thrill, that high motivation to travel across uncharted land is what we want you to think about when you think excitement and your Why It Matters journey. Conjure up times when you are fulfilled, happy, motivated.

Excitement stems from being intrinsically motivated to pursue an activity at a high level at your leisure. Nothing is driving you externally to commit to the action. Your own inner interest carries you. You don't need any obvious external rewards. You simply enjoy something, or see it as a way to explore, to learn, to be a better person.

On our compass, the West, **Excitement** focuses on:

What drives you?
What fulfills you?
What satisfies you?
What motivates you?

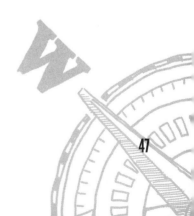

Reflect on situations over the course of your life, and think of visible signs of **Excitement**: Think about when…

…your heart beats faster.
…your voice shows intensity.
…you just plain feel good.

What caused you to have this heightened state of being fully alive?

Excitement leads you to do what you want to do. You will be happy, exuberant, content, and satisfied when you are motivated and fulfilled. **Excitement** leads you to do certain things. Your Why It Matters will lead you to behave in certain ways. It is the inner drive to act the way you do.

Examining what gives you **Excitement** will help you identify your Why It Matters. This is uniquely personal. Let's explore further:

NAME: LAQUANDA
OCCUPATION: ENGINEER
AGE: 36
LOCATION: OHIO, USA
WHY IT MATTERS: TO PREPARE

At the end of a work day, when I am using my strengths and am 'on my game,' I experience an extreme sense of satisfaction. Let's say that I was totally prepared for a presentation, and I was great. This is really a thrill for me. It puts a smile on my face and a bounce in my step.

Moving from work back home is seamless when I am operating in this mode. My family reaps the results of my happiness. I have dinner prepared. All the kids are organized with their sports. Excitement leads to satisfaction.

We are drawn to things that work for us. We get a thrill when everything goes right. When we are using our strengths, we are happier. We are excited. We are motivated. We would go as far to say, find out when you get 'giddy.' Giddy means 'joyfully elated.' That is what happens when you are doing what excites you. That is when your Why It Matters appears, close to the surface, so it's easy to identify.

Your motivator, your Why It Matters is not your passion, your purpose, or your calling. Let's think about these concepts.

Passion centers on the contribution you make to the world. It is about what you need to do. Passion leads to action. It is what you are excited about doing for your own self-actualization. Your passion is what you truly love to do. You can find your passion by figuring out what you love. Your passion is intuitive. It is where you feel yourself to be happiest.

Your **purpose** is similar, but it is more focused on answering the question of "Why am I here?" In a spiritual sense, finding your purpose relates to why your God put you on this planet: to do what you are supposed do. When you find your purpose, all the stars are aligned, and you can experience fulfillment.

YOUR PASSION AND PURPOSE ARE A RESULT OF YOUR WHY IT MATTERS.

Your **calling** is a mission, a job to be done. It is the answer to the question of "What should I be when I grow up?" It is a job that fits, a place you enjoy. It is much more related to passion than Why It Matters.

Purpose, passion, and calling are acts of doing, Why It Matters just is. Why It Matters will bring you fulfillment because of the knowledge and identification of what it is, not the doing of it.

Your Why It Matters is not your passion or your purpose. **However, it must be said, your passion and purpose are a result of your Why It Matter**s.

Find what excites you, and you get closer to who you are and what you are made of. Read the questions that follow. Read slowly. Try to answer each one with some real thought. If you are stuck, just skip a question, and move on to the next one. It is an exercise in personal brainstorming.

What does my day look like when I experiencing happiness?
What does fulfillment look like for me?
When am I most excited during the day?
What challenges me?
What do I want to learn more about? What do I know a lot about?
What is important to me?
What am I determined to do, no matter what?
What do I offer the world, personally and professionally?
At the end of each day, what tells me that I had a great day?

Excitement means:

_____

_____

Transfer to page 67 to have your story all on one page.

Now that you have a few answers, let's look at some examples. For a given set of motivators, we'll share an actual Why It Matters. You will start to see how the facts you are gathering about yourself start to translate into that essential phrase: your **Why It Matters**.

FOR SOMEONE WHO IS FULFILLED OR THRILLED BY:	WHY IT MATTERS MIGHT BE:
• Challenges. • Completing a big project. • Putting the last piece in a jigsaw puzzle. • Reading the last page in a book.	**To complete** **To get it done**
• Someone saying I did a good job. • Knowing people have appreciated the work I did. • My kids telling me that I am the best Dad in the world.	**To be recognized** **To be accepted**
• Connecting everyone in a group I am working with. • Accomplishing tasks that people did not think I could do. • Finding a way to stretch my resources in some creative way.	**To fill the gap** **To connect**
• When people agree with me during a meeting. • When I can change someone's mind, it makes my day. • I love it when I can be a mentor to someone.	**To be heard** **To be understood**

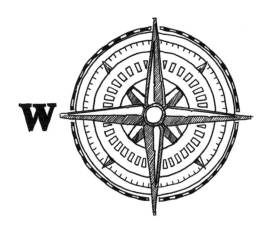

NAME: ROBIN
OCCUPATION: HEALTH ASSESSOR
AGE: 40
LOCATION: GAUTENG, SOUTH AFRICA
WHY IT MATTERS: TO CONNECT

A conversation with an executive coach:

Coach: *What drives your choices? What gets you excited?*

Robin: *More than anything, what is happening with my kids, I am passionate about my children. In the morning I review all I have to do during the day. I focus on bringing my kids to their first day of soccer, on the positive aspects of meeting a new client. I am excited about those two things because I will get to connect to a new person and my kids will connect to a new coach and new teammates. So really it's not my kids that drive me as much as seeing them connect to new people and experiences.*

Coach: *Robin, you are a connector yourself. Your Why It Matters is to connect or to make a connection. How does having this information change your life? How does knowing this help you?*

Robin: *First, I know that if I make the effort to connect with someone or help two people connect with each other, I am going to be happy. Second, If I am able to 'connect the dots' as part of a project or a plan, I will be able to move forward and be successful. I really can't move forward if things don't connect; it is when my weaknesses appear. I will push way too hard. I will push a square peg into a round hole just to create a connection. I know how to avoid that now*

A conversation with an executive coach:

Coach: *What are you determined to do, no matter what?*

Ric: *I am determined to finish everything I start. If I start something, it has to be important because I know I am going to take it all the way to a conclusion. I must solve it. I do not care what obstacles get in the way. I will find a solution and solve the problem. I am obsessed with solving it. For me, life is all about problem solving, and the more problems I can solve, the better I am as a person.*

Why It Matters allows you to discover truth. Your Why It Matters is the same no matter what job you have. Whether you are working as a CEO or as a server in a fast food restaurant, your Why It Matters will be the same. Your Why It Matters does not change.

YOUR WHY IT MATTERS DOES NOT CHANGE.

Knowing your Why It Matters leaves you with acknowledgement and understanding of who you are. You know how to handle things better because you know what motivates you. Knowing what really motivates you allows you to avoid situations in which you won't find any satisfaction.

EAST: ESSENCE

The final point of the compass is **Essence**. The east on our compass brings to mind the mystic Far East. This will be a philosophical look at your Why It Matters. It is a deeper look at yourself, at…

…your heart
…your spirit
…your core

Picture yourself wearing an invisible cloak, called your Essence. It goes everywhere with you. Your Essence is your constant state of being that is constantly 'on,' always functioning, whether you are aware of it or not. Your Essence is that internal motor that propels you and keeps you going full throttle all day.

Computers have operating systems: motors that run behind the scenes while you are busy running applications. You have an internal operating system, too. It is your Essence. Your Essence runs concurrently behind the scenes. It usually goes unnoticed, but it constantly influences your behavior.

You can describe your Essence as your brand. It is what people have come to expect from you. Everyone around you knows you and knows how you will react. It is what you bring to people. Your brand. It just shows up no matter what, in both good and bad times. Your Essence is constant and unchanging. It is your first reaction. Your Essence is something you have had in your mind for so long that it is literally burned into your brain.

NAME: JONAS
OCCUPATION: SUPPLY CHAIN DIRECTOR
AGE: 39
LOCATION: PUEBLO, MEXICO
WHY IT MATTERS: TO GET IT DONE

Jonas does the work. He knows his business inside and out. When things don't go well, when fill rates are too low, when the distribution center has delays, he flies into a fit of frustration. Everyone knows to stay out of his way. Everyone knows that he needs a couple of hours to cool off. Everyone knows that talking to him at this time is a waste of time. Jonas has clearly shared his 'brand.' His essence is fiery, and that is very clear to everyone around him, that he has to get it done (or else).

Justin Kennedy, our South African chief executive and professor in neuroscience, talks about Essence: "With the proper knowledge and training, you can use your conscious mind to change your physical brain. Really change it, so the way you think, the way you act, and the way you feel can all be made better." He tells us about neuroplasticity, which refers

THE WAY YOU THINK, THE WAY YOU ACT, AND THE WAY YOU FEEL CAN ALL BE MADE BETTER.

to the brain's ability to change and adapt. You really are in control, and you really do have choices. When you think new thoughts, you are actually changing the geography of your brain, changing the electric patterns that create and carry thoughts, changing the chemicals that control moods and energy levels.

55

You know how to tie your shoes, but you didn't get it right the first time you tried. As a child, you learned it and did it many times over until it was second nature. As an adult, a coach can help you develop different reactions to people and situations, reduce stress, and develop more and more flexibility in your thought patterns as your mind begins to work without stress, until it becomes as natural to you as tying your shoes.

You strengthen the parts of the brain that you exercise. A study in London proves how much we can change our brains. The streets of London are a modern-day mess, designed by the ancient Romans. A taxi driver in London has to hold an incredibly complex map in his memory. It takes two years or more to study and learn the system. During that time, the part of the driver's brain that deals with knowledge and memory actually gets larger. The way you think improves your ability to think that way. As you discover Why It Matters, the discovery process you are going through is changing the way you think and how you make choices.

When patterns in your behavior are repeated, they become an integral part of who you are. They become essential. You can choose to run your life and make your own choices, or you can let others run your life for you. Become aware of your thinking and realize you can make your own choices.

By asking yourself questions, by thinking about your own thought process, you might begin to see patterns. You say 'yes' to certain things and 'no' to others. When you make a choice, stop. Push the 'pause' button, and consider the thoughts that led you to your final decision. By reflecting and pausing, you might detect what internal power or force is pushing you to make the choices you make.

Reflection takes practice. Stop. Think about what is going on with your own internal operating system. Once you discover your Essence, you will see if this internal power is working for you or against you. When you are thoughtful and in control, your Essence can guide you to greatness.

NAME: BOB
OCCUPATION: VP OF ENGINEERING
AGE: 45
LOCATION: ARIZONA, USA
WHY IT MATTERS: TO ADD VALUE

Bob tries to have his way every time he opens his mouth. He tells his wife on Thanksgiving Day, 'This would make the gravy taste better.' This does not necessarily help his wife in the kitchen as she is finishing up the Thanksgiving meal. Working with his direct reports when they are figuring out a complex project, Bob will say, "Those are all fine ideas, but I think you should do this instead ..." His people look at each other and shrug their shoulders.

He doesn't even stop and think about it. He just does it. Many times it has worked. Bob is an exceptional engineer. But as you can guess, sometimes it just doesn't work.

Bob wants to add value. He is really sincere about it. He wants to make sure people see that he can add value and does to any situation. That is Bob's Essence, to add value. It is always present.

Let's push the 'pause' button for long enough to stop to think about the following:

- *How would you describe your Essence?*
- *What 'constant-on' state do you have behind the scenes?*
- *What behavior shows up a lot without being invited?*

You might have several words that come to your mind or you might have to do some heavy critical thinking.

Your ideas:

_____

_____

_____

Transfer to page 67 to have your story all on one page.

The point of all this is simple.

If you reflect, learn, and study, you improve your ability to think clearly and live a better life.

If you spend time sorting things out and understanding yourself in a completely new way, you will be a better person.

The more you live without stress, the more you will find yourself feeling flexible, creative, and happy.

COMBINE

You are now ready to do your own deep dive into finding and identifying your Why It Matters. You have everything you need for success.

Your Why It Matters is what drives you, your internal roadmap, your inner GPS. There are four ways to make your search easier and find your Why It Matters.

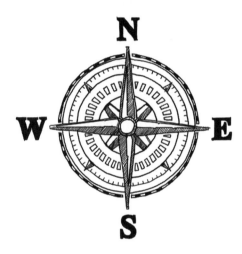

North: Exposure is what is ingrained in your experience.
South: Evidence is your shield, your armor, your good and bad.
West: Excitement is what fulfills and thrills you.
East: Essence is your internal guide and spirit.

If you have any other questions, any other thoughts around finding your Why It Matters. This chapter should answer every last one of them.

Benefits of knowing your Why It Matters:

PLEASURE & PAIN

The two big reasons for knowing and owning your Why It Matters are these: pleasure and pain. Pleasure and pain are the embodiment of motivators. Neuroscience and your own experience have proven that you will always move toward pleasure and away from pain. You are wired to seek pleasure and disconnect from pain.

Learning your Why It Matters will move you toward pleasure. It will provide pleasure by maintaining a peaceful balance in life. It opens up opportunity for rewards.

On the other hand, it will also keep you away from pain. When your Why It Matters runs amok, your relationships weaken. Your situations become more challenging. You experience discomfort. You feel pain.

NEW LEARNING

- *Helps you choose things in which you will be successful.*
- *Gives you a vantage point from which you can be self aware.*
- *Allows you to accept yourself the way you are and forgive yourself for things that do not go well.*
- *Allows you to explain yourself and create better relationships.*
- *Helps you step away from potential conflicts.*

NEW RESULTS

- *Teaching your children from your own experience.*
- *Looking at yourself differently in your current relationships.*
- *Connecting to new relationships.*
- *Using your time more effectively.*
- *Validating yourself in front of others.*
- *Choosing your battles.*
- *Constructing meaning in things.*
- *Making positive choices when deciding on a behavior to use.*
- *Understanding your blind spots.*

YOUR JOB

Do you want to guide your career to a place that makes you feel excited, enthusiastic, and motivated? These questions will help you figure out whether you are in the right place. Think about your current job. **With each question, look beyond the details of what you do; focus on who you are.**

What do I like most about working?

_____

_____

If I don't do this during the day in a job, I am not happy:

_____

_____

This makes me happy at work:

_____

_____

Success in a work day looks like:

_____

_____

What does my future look like? What excites me about the opportunities?

_____

_____

What do I want to learn?

_____

_____

What do I want more of in a job?

_____

_____

What would provide peace for me in a job?

_____

_____

HELPFUL HINTS

To define your Why It Matters, you will need to be specific and personal. Everyone wants to leave a legacy. You can do that, of course. Your Why It Matters is not something you share in common with everyone else. Why It Matters is not something that just happens. It is an accumulation of all your experiences, thoughts, and ideas.

Avoid clichés. Stay away from things other people say are important. Identify things that truly resonate with you. Be genuine. If you want it to sound noble, you might come up with statements about your Why It Matters like this:

- *I want to make a difference.*
- *I want to help people.*
- *I want to support my family.*
- *I want people to remember me.*

These are all good and noble thoughts, but they don't provide your Why It Matters. These are the results of your Why It Matters. You make a difference when your Why It Matters is in full working order.

Here are a few things that might get in the way of naming your Why It Matters:

- *It can sound egotistical when you say it out loud.*
- *The process of naming it might 'feel' contrived.*
- *Reflecting might be uncomfortable for you.*
- *It takes work.*
- *It takes time.*
- *It might be hard to figure out.*
- *You might not like the result.*

Your answer won't necessarily come to you immediately. It might come to you at the strangest and most fortuitous time.

WHY IT MATTERS EXAMPLES

To accomplish
To adapt
To adjust
To anticipate
To appear knowledgeable
To avoid failure
To be a catalyst
To be a dominant force
To be a guiding light
To be accepted
To be better than average
To be comfortable
To be considered the expert
To be included
To be loved
To be noticed
To be perfect
To be recognized
To be relevant
To be respected

To be safe
To be secure
To be the focal point
To be the hero
To be understood
To be worthwhile
To belong
To connect
To contemplate
To finish
To judge
To make things right
To nurture
To protect
To prove my competence
To satisfy
To serve
To stay in my comfort zone
To teach
To win

FINDING MY WHY IT MATTERS

Now it is your turn to put all four points of the compass together and to be the subject and scientist in determining your own Why It Matters. Meticulously piece together your exposure, evidence, essence and excitement. The work you have done so far can be brought to this page, so you can see it all in one place:

What is your life story telling you?

EXPOSURE

VALUES

_____

_____

_____

EVIDENCE

STRENGTHS   **WEAKNESSES**

_____   _____

_____   _____

_____   _____

WORDS AND STORIES I USE

_____

_____

_____

EXCITEMENT

_____

_____

_____

ESSENCE

_____

_____

_____

MY WHY IT MATTERS IS:

_____

AM I RIGHT?

A checklist for your Why It Matters:

1. Your 'weaknesses' are your Why It Matters run amok. To validate your Why It Matters, simply see whether your weaknesses are connected to your Why It Matters as it is stated. Look at your weaknesses. Do they appear when your Why It Matters is threatened or cornered?

2. You know you have it right if you 'own' it and can defend it. You have to be comfortable as the owner of the word or phrase you have come up with. You have to be okay with it.

3. This is a personal journey. Your Why It Matters must be clear to you, even if others might disagree about it. It has to be something you can embrace. It has to be a word that resonates with you. It has to make perfect sense when you say it and when you explain it.

Circle your answers as you ask yourself:

Do I 'own' it?	YES	NO
Am I okay with it?	YES	NO
Am I able to push back if someone disagrees?	YES	NO
Can I clearly explain it?	YES	NO
Does my behavior consistently connect to it?	YES	NO

WHY IT MATTERS: BRENDA TO BE OF SERVICE

NORTH-EXPOSURE:

My Why It Matters, like everyone else's, goes back a long time. I don't remember not volunteering. The earliest I remember serving others is at the age of 12. In my native Canada, I volunteered in the burn treatment unit at the Montreal Hospital. The unit served children with severe burns. Most could not move from their beds. Many had to stay in one position, often face down. These children were in pain. My job was to bring them joy. I would scoot under their beds to look up at their faces. I read to them, and we spoke in French. I played for hours at a time on the floor with these wonderful children. I loved making their day, making them laugh, and helping them forget their pain for a minute.

Then in high school, I worked at an 'old men's home,' as it was called. I worked serving the men their dinner. We played backgammon, chess, and checkers. For a young girl, it was unnerving to begin with, but eventually, I had 50 new grandpas. Serving them felt so natural to me.

MY WHY IT MATTERS, LIKE EVERYONE ELSE'S, GOES BACK A LONG TIME.

I went to college and entered the fields of kinesiology and psychology. I served autistic children and emotionally disturbed teenagers. Over time, I found that my true calling was with older adults. I worked in long-term care for many years. I never stopped serving.

I have volunteered as a 'big sister' with the Big Sisters Association in Canada. My Little Sister and I have been together for over 30 years. We grew up together. No matter what she was dealing with, I was there for her. She was there at the birth of my daughter, Dani, and she was there at Dani's wedding last year. I have served her since we met.

I have always 'been of service' as a mother to my children and now to their spouses. My favorite assignment is serving my husband. I want him to be happy, so I serve, whether he wants me to or not.

A number of years ago, I was on the phone with my mother in Canada; it was one of our last conversations together. She said to me, "Brenda, don't ever ask how I am feeling again. Ask about the weather. Ask about the neighbors. Just don't ask about my health." I was at a loss. I was comfortable asking about her health. That allowed me to serve, but she took that away from me. If I didn't serve her, how could I communicate with her? You see, asking about neighbors is not serving. I had trouble ever speaking to her again.

SOUTH - EVIDENCE:

Strengths

- *I am a good teacher.*
- *I am patient. I serve and continue serving until you have what you need.*
- *I will do just about anything for anyone.*

Weaknesses

- *I serve even if you don't want me to.*
- *I can serve without truly being a servant.*

Imagine I am at your house for an enjoyable dinner. If I can't serve, I can fall apart. Without really being invited, I will help you serve dinner. I get people drinks. I bring people appetizers even if they are within easy reach. As you can imagine, this behavior is not always welcome.

I am a coach, so I serve my clients. I am a parent, so I serve my kids. I am a wife, so I serve my husband. That's where my weakness hides; I will be of service, but I will not be a servant. Sometimes I serve in order to be in control.

I have been told that when I can't serve someone, I will shut down. One brilliant young woman named Erica said to me, "Brenda, when you stop serving, you shut down. It is as if you fall off the edge of the cliff." It's true. I can shut down quite easily at a cocktail party or social event. I have observed, and I have changed my behavior. I make a big effort to listen to whoever is in front of me, no matter what the topic.

When it comes to words I use and stories I tell, there is one strong example I can share: Bringing up my children, my favorite word was 'kindness.' Kindness and service go hand in hand. The stories we shared with our children were surrounded in service. We volunteered serving at a Christmas dinner, something our entire family did for a decade. We volunteered as a family at an animal shelter. That is how my kids grew up.

EAST - ESSENCE:
My essence is all about service. I see a homeless man, and I don't want to give him the shirt off my back. I don't want to give him money. I want to sit him down and help him write his resume and prepare for a job interview. It's just what I do.

WEST - EXCITEMENT:
To be of service is what I do, no matter what happens. I get a thrill when I serve someone, and it makes their lives better. My motivation, my enthusiasm, my focus around being of service is simple and straightforward. As you can imagine, in the long-term care arena, there are a lot of us who serve. The jobs I have chosen, from Alzheimer's to autism to executive coaching, are all focused around being of service. It is my motivator. It is more than my passion or purpose. **It is my Why It Matters.**

WHY IT MATTERS: KARL TO PROVIDE ACCOMPLISHMENTS

My Why It Matters is "to provide accomplishments." If my Why It Matters is not perfect, it's pretty close. I love doing things for people, above everything else.

NORTH - EXPOSURE:

Growing up, I had my Mom and my Dad as role models. They were both very serious about what they did for a living, and I took them seriously.

My Mom was a classical pianist. As a teenager, she did a tour of Europe with one of the world's leading violinists. Classical music operates in a very rigid set of rules and still allows for passion, even genius, to shine through.

IF MY WHY IT MATTERS IS NOT PERFECT, IT'S PRETTY CLOSE.

My Dad was a journalist, a pioneer in radio news. Coming out of a small Ohio town, his news department won national honors, beating out stations in New York, Chicago, and L.A. Reporters work under the banner of accuracy, and the restraints of writing style, but they, too, have a lot of freedom for self-expression.

Every time my Dad moved to a new job, a new radio station, we moved to a new city. I learned how to adapt, and I learned how to make new friends on a regular basis. Again, I had to please an audience. I couldn't stay in a comfort zone and do what I felt like doing. I had to deliver what other people needed in order to get along. When I figured out my audience and delivered the right lines, made the right moves, it just worked.

Getting things accomplished. That was a constant message I taught to my children. Whether it was their nightly homework or earning their college degree, they learned from a young age that doing it and finishing it was what mattered in life.

SOUTH - EVIDENCE:

I am all about getting things done. I don't sit around. I have been successful at running my own business for 30 years. When I come up with an idea or an answer to someone's question, I can't wait to tell them about it. When I fulfill a promise, I get a lot of satisfaction from getting it done. I work for my audience. I have a strong drive to get things done for people. That creates some strengths and leads to my weaknesses, too.

Strengths
- *I do the work. Anything you ask of me will get done.*
- *I am effective and efficient. I demand a lot of myself in the way of quality.*
- *I judge the quality of my own accomplishments; I rarely seek approval, and I rarely take things personally.*

All this allows me to make decisions, set my own direction, and get to the results. No unfinished projects or false starts. There is a drive to accomplish, and people have to be involved. I need results that speak to what someone wants or needs. It is rare that I do something just for myself.

Weaknesses
I can miss the mark. I will accomplish something without placing it in context. I'll get up after dinner and clear the dishes, even in the middle of an intimate conversation. You have probably heard it said, "Women want to be heard. Men need to provide an answer." That applies to me. I am not good at 'just listening.' If I think I know what you need, I will stop listening and start doing, even if I'm entirely wrong about what you want me to do.

The stories I tell will describe end results rather than how something happened or why I thought it was important in the first place. The words I use can include "Let's do it!"

EAST - ESSENCE:

I provide accomplishments all the time. I package things. I deliver them to people. I could have gone my whole life without someone pointing this out to me. Now that they have, I understand myself a lot better. I can avoid acting out my weaknesses because I can see them coming a mile away.

I know how to be happy. Doing things for others is in perfect harmony with my faith. My parents taught me to work hard and be serious about it, but somehow, to share it with someone. I share my parents' values. It's natural for me.

WEST - EXCITEMENT:

I was born in the right era to live out my passion: playing rock and roll. With my mother being a classical pianist, I grew up with music around the house and music flowing through my veins. From the time I was 5 years old, I wanted to be a drummer.

The drummer isn't out front playing solos or singing lead vocals. The drummer sits on the 'second line,' keeping the band together, cueing up the next song, laying down the beat. I still play drums, and I love it.

Like my Dad, I gather information and then put it together for delivery. I am a researcher with an annual market survey that's well known in my industry. I live out my Why It Matters in a huge way when 20,000 people read my report every year. I am providing for them.

Knowing my Why It Matters makes me self-aware. I stop. I apply what I know about myself to what I want to do. It allows me to hold on, take more time, and make better decisions.

WHY IT MATTERS: JENNIFER TO PROVE MY WORTH

NORTH-EXPOSURE:

Being an only child has its pros and cons. One of the benefits was getting my parents' full attention. The problem was that I got all of their attention, all the time.

When I was 6 years old, I remember being in the grocery store with my mother. It was a blazing hot summer day. I could not wait to get inside to air-conditioned comfort. As we walked up and down the aisles, I drifted to the front of the grocery store and saw what I thought were free brochures. I was an avid reader. I liked flashy pictures and food. The brochure contained both. As I walked back to find my mom, I put the brochure in my pocket. We checked out and spent a minute chatting with the store manager, Miss Penny. My mother was determined to make the drive home before our ice cream melted. As we drove, I excitedly pulled out the "free brochure." My mom asked where I got the recipe book. I told her.

Turning the car around must have been hard for my mother on that blazing hot day, but she valued honesty more than ice cream. It was a long walk back into the grocery store to confess what I did to Miss Penny. It was a lesson I have not forgotten. I learned something important about my mother that day. My mom is now a Chief Financial Officer. Her honesty has served her well.

My Why It Matters. "to prove my worth," was also starting to emerge. I took the brightly colored recipe book, so I could give my mother a gift and prove my worth.

One day, in elementary school, I came home from school visibly upset. I barreled through the front door and began screaming for my mother. I proceeded to tell her that the cafeteria monitor called me a 'busy body.' I did not know what the word meant, but I did know by the tone of her voice that it wasn't a good thing.

Mom told me a 'busy body' was someone who sticks their nose in other people's business. I told her that I was just trying to help two friends out that were having an argument. I told her I was trying 'to help,' but all I was really doing was proving my worth.

SOUTH-EVIDENCE:
Strengths
- *I am goal oriented and like to produce results.*
- *I am driven by getting things done and items crossed off my to-do list. I work at a fast pace.*
- *I build solid working relationships because people trust me to get things done. They can count on me.*

Weaknesses
- *I can 'drop the ball' when trying to maintain so many relationships.*
- *I sometime fail to follow through on things, especially with people who already know my worth.*
- *When I am not sure how to get to a solid result, I can be impulsive, or I can get lost in the details. These things seem to be opposites, but they are driven by the same thing.*

Words and Stories:
I often use words such as "Let me tell you about a time..." or "Have you heard of ...?"

I notice I share the same stories over and over. Most of these stories have a common theme: my achievements, what validates my value or my expertise.

I tell my children how important education is. I talk about the books I read and the things I know. When someone tells me something regarding an experience or a situation, I most often validate what they are telling me with my own experience or things I have read. Again, I am proving my worth by validating their contributions.

EAST-ESSENCE:

This Why It Matters of mine is unique to me and my experiences. I tend to prove my worth at all costs. That is what gets me up in the morning and helps me determine at the end of the day what success looked like.

I don't need an invitation to prove my worth. I can spend an incredible amount of emotional energy trying to prove my worth to someone who doesn't care. I can feel hurt if I need to withhold support and let someone work things out by themselves.

My faith has also showed me that the only one I need to prove my worth to is my maker. He has already affirmed that I am worthy. Some days, I still can't believe it.

WEST-EXCITEMENT:

I am a teacher at heart. Excitement for me is helping others succeed by being the one person that can reliably give them what they need in the moment. It might be providing new information, giving my recommendation, or helping them work through their best ideas.

I love proving my worth to others. I also need to prove it to myself. I like to challenge myself physically and mentally. I set goals and meet them, so I can prove to myself that I am important, valuable, worthy. At the end of it all, the thrill is the opinion more than the accomplishment.

WHY IT MATTERS: LARRY TO POLICE

NORTH-EXPOSURE:

At the age of 7, I was diagnosed with bone cancer. I lost my left leg. I did not ask for this to happen, but it did. I had to navigate my life very differently starting at the age of 7.

My mother supported me every step of the way. Her traditional Eastern European upbringing taught her how to protect, defend, and escort me through my youth. She was my private police force, a source of law and order, and a fairly tight limiting factor if I wanted to try something that involved risk.

I ALWAYS FELT THAT I NEEDED TO BE BETTER THAN MY PEERS.

I always felt that I needed to be better than my peers. I did this through asserting myself into everything. I wanted it to be known that despite my disability, I was on the same playing field with my peers. Just like a policeman, I would investigate a situation and stake out a way to make my circumstances work.

In junior high school, I was determined to show everyone I could win the Presidential Physical Fitness Award just like any other top competitor. I ended up with results in the 95th percentile. That year, the physical education department selected me as the Physical Education Student of the Year. The entire student body gave me a standing ovation as I walked across the stage that day to accept my award. I was proud that I could show my peers that I was capable of doing most of what they could, and in some cases, do it better. It was a true victory, I had won the battle.

SOUTH-EVIDENCE:

If I want to do something, I do it. I make my list, set my eyes on the prize, and go for it. Roads may be blocked, but that never deters me from getting things done. I take control, like an army of one.

Looking back on my own actions and the way I behave, I definitely can see a pattern. I assert myself in my relationships, at work, and in my personal life. If I do not agree with something or someone, I will let it be known. I analyze situations. I constantly "police" every situation. I do not have a problem with crucial conversations or being bold in situations.

Looking at my strengths and weaknesses, you can definitely see a story being told.

My strengths: determination, focus, and persistence. I make the rules. I cannot be forced to give up. I will not accept 'no' as a final answer. I will interrogate my sources and judge their responses. I will keep going if I want a different answer from a different source.

My weaknesses: being impatient, being critical, and being the perfectionist. I like things moving quickly and moving in my direction. My judgment comes into play in almost everything I do. I am also a perfectionist. Things need to be exactly right and kept in their place. I am more of a perfectionist with my environment than I am with end results.

The stories I tell usually involve how I found an operational improvement or how I have helped the community by policing, making necessary changes, and letting people know they were made.

These weaknesses can lead me to be skeptical of folks taking a risk or trying something new. My words most often reflect my opinion, for better or worse.

EAST-ESSENCE:

I police and monitor my relationships and my environment automatically, all the time. I constantly scan and judge to see whether there is a more efficient way of doing something. If I find a more efficient way, I make it known, whether my opinion was requested or not. In fact, I offer up my opinion more often than not. Sometimes it is a good thing, and sometimes it is not.

I defend, support, and stand up for those things I value. I assert myself. I step in if there is a need.

I am an amputee, so my physical existence has always been 'front and center.' I police what goes into my body. I am on a self-imposed diet. If I become overweight, I only have one knee joint to support the weight of my body. I am diligent about what goes into my body and the way I exercise. I am extreme in the way I police myself.

WEST-EXCITEMENT:

I can say it has been a great day when I have taken care of everything on my 'to do' list.

I am a concrete thinker. I like to see things get done. When there is a roadblock or obstacle in the way of my achieving, then I police the situation and assert myself to find out what might need to be done.

This might result in anger when something gets in my way. When my rules don't apply or my mission is thwarted, I can become agitated. I get stressed. I can come across as pushy and demanding.

I go out of my way to make sure people are protected. If you ask my wife, she would say that I like to make my presence known and make sure I have policed just about every situation.

My Why It Matters, "to police," is me to the core. Now that I know what it is, I know when I need to let some things go and not insist on things going my way.

FINDING WHY IT MATTERS: PENNY

Now that you have heard four people share their stories, we will try to draw out deeper answers in a series of interviews. We call this the Coaching Perspective.

NAME: PENNY
OCCUPATION: DIETICIAN
AGE: 44
LOCATION: KENT, ENGLAND
WHY IT MATTERS: TO BE LIKED

Penny, what do you remember about your childhood that stands out to help us find your Why It Matters?

My earliest memory as a child was wanting to fit in. I wanted to blend in. I didn't want to stand out in any way. I had no idea why I was this way. My brothers weren't this way. They were bold and strong. They didn't worry what other people thought or said. Not me. I worried how I would fit in. Don't shine the spotlight on me. Don't single me out in class.

What did 'fitting in' look like?

If the world around me was happy, then so was I. Wanting to fit in meant that I never heard anything unkind said about me. I certainly never wanted to get in trouble as a kid. It is so vivid to me. I would do anything in my power to avoid my parents' disappointment. This drove me so strongly…my whole childhood.

Any other stories that you remember?

At the beginning of the school year, I was riding the bus with my brothers for the first time. When I got on the bus, I sat next to my brother, and the entire bus laughed. I will never forget that moment. Why were they laughing? Were they laughing at me? Where else would I sit except next to my brother? As it turns out, there was a rule: boys on one side, girls on the other. How was I to know? I was humiliated. I don't know why this was so important – it just was. I never walked on the bus again without sitting in the right place. I make sure I do what it takes to be liked, anywhere and everywhere.

What do you say to your kids?

I tell my children to work hard at being caring and that if you are caring, the rest will fall into place.

Tell me what motivates you. What is exciting for you?

The most exciting thing in my life is when people are around me, and they are happy and pleased with what I can give them and what I can do for them. My biggest thrill is when I leave an encounter and I know I was well-received.

Okay, so let's look at your strengths and weaknesses. You have spent a lot of time reflecting about these two areas. Can you share the results with me?

Strengths: I will talk with anyone. I really am friendly. I like to know people's stories. This works well in most environments. This is a gift, and I cannot think of a time that talking with people has been a negative. This trait has gotten me far and has been a perfect complement to my career path.

Weaknesses: People want to know why I am always in a good mood. People get irritated at times because they think I am pushing my happiness and kindness on them. People say to me, "Can't you dial down that exuberance? You cannot possibly be sincere." I fall apart when that happens.

Anything else?

Sometimes I wonder if my desire to be liked came from wanting to avoid conflict or if I avoided conflict because of my Why It Matters. Which came first? The two are certainly wrapped around each other. They work together.

What is your favorite word?

My favorite word is 'care.' I use it with my clients, my husband, and my children. I use it every day.

What about your essence? What do you do no matter what?

My being liked is a part of me. I can't do anything without the security of the people around me liking me. It will be a show stopper if I have the vibes that someone in the group does not like me. I have to go and fix 'that' and then move on with my activities.

Being liked. It is part of who I am, and it's always been there. It is as inherent in me as my eye color, and I like it. I am outgoing. I love people. I can talk with anyone. Thanks for talking with me. I hope you like what I told you.

FINDING WHY IT MATTERS:
KATHY

NAME: KATHY
OCCUPATION: SOCIAL WORKER
AGE: 41
LOCATION: ONTARIO, CANADA
WHY IT MATTERS: TO RESCUE

Kathy, how has your past molded you?

I still remember something that shaped who I am today. On my way home from my first day of school I found a lost kitten. I went door to door with this kitten and begged people to 'adopt' her. After a very unsuccessful day, I brought the kitten home. My mother would not permit the kitten to stay. We had to take her to the shelter and to this day I cannot set foot in an animal shelter.

What did you learn from that experience?

All I wanted was to rescue the kitten. I totally failed and I could barely live with myself. Rescuing became my life. A few years later, I found out that a friend was being beaten by her mother. I was really upset. I begged my mom to intervene. My mother said that it was not her place. Then, I begged my friend to get help from the school counselor.

How did this play out?

I spent many sleepless nights and shed some tears about this. Eventually, I told my teacher what was happening. My friend was furious. She never spoke to me again.

What theme can you see in these stories?

I try to rescue anyone or anything from their situations or circumstances.

What do you do, no matter what? Your essence?

I think about how to rescue people. That goes on, no matter what they need to be rescued from. That goes on, whether they want rescuing or not. It can be something big, like I told you about. It can be something small. I will try to save somebody if they are asked to offer an opinion in a meeting, and they don't want to. I'll rescue people from having to answer a difficult question, even if I am the one who asked it. It is always running through me. It is my constant "on" state.

Let's go back to look at your strengths and weaknesses. Can you tell me about them?

My strength is I am direct and do not beat around the bush. People hear truth from me. They do not ever wonder what I am thinking or how I am feeling about a situation. I am very focused and can solve any problem in front of me. My weaknesses will not surprise you, I rescue all the time. People around me cannot make their own decision.

What do you do that really gets you excited?

I like to discover things. I like to find things that no one else has found. I also get a kick out of recovering lost projects or items. I save things from being ignored or neglected.

What words or stories do you repeat often?

"Saves" is my favorite word. From saving some "me time," you know, rescuing myself, to saving a puppy. Save, save, save. That's who I am.

PEOPLE WHO FOUND WHAT THEY WERE LOOKING FOR

You have looked deeply into the four points on your compass: **Exposure, Evidence, Excitement**, and **Essence**. You have a good idea what your Why It Matters is. Knowing this information, your Why It Matters, clearly gives you insight into yourself. It gives you a different entry point for understanding yourself. It's a gem, a diamond.

Now you can answer the question: "Why do I do the things I do?" It's something you would not have discovered without this book, the time you took to read it, and the time you took to work with it. This knowledge truly is power, as long as you act on it.

The next question is: *now what*? What will your plan be?

Reflect. You must decide what to do with this new knowledge. Begin by bringing deliberate thought and strategic action to all of your behaviors. To change your life, you first have to change your behavior. Examine the behaviors that can be changed from this new knowledge.

Allow this knowledge to make a difference for you in the tough spots. Choose your communication and your reaction to communication in a more thoughtful way.

Earlier, we talked about running from here to there, running on 'autopilot,' failing to be present "in the moment." By identifying and recognizing your exposure, evidence, excitement, and essence, you can now take yourself off autopilot. You can remove some of the hard wiring that caused you to react the way you did prior to finding your Why It Matters.

You now have the power to make the best decisions moving forward.

Please join us on this final ascent to your personal summit by reading true accounts, true stories from people who know what you now know. These folks have changed their behavior and changed their lives because of this new knowledge.

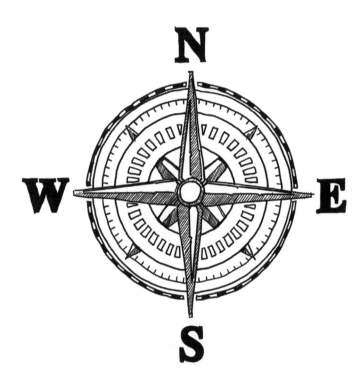

I have always been a quick responder. This mode of operating has followed me throughout my life. My Why It Matters is "to provide a quick response." I didn't think that was very flattering. Coming to grips with the reality was the first step I had to take in order to change the way I behave.

I have been operating this way for as long as I can remember. I provide a quick response when asked a question. I provide a quick response when asked to do something; I provide a quick response in everything I do. Taking action too quickly cost me friendships and promotions at work. I rarely took time, gathered the facts, and slowed down to process things. Now that I have discovered my Why It Matters, I have learned to slow down and think carefully before deciding what to say or do.

Discovering my Why It Matters has truly been a revelation for me. I recently received the promotion I desired.

NAME: DON
OCCUPATION: HUMAN RESOURCE MANAGER
AGE: 46
LOCATION: FREE STATE, SOUTH AFRICA
WHY IT MATTERS: TO FIGURE IT OUT

Wow, to think that four little words could make such an impact was beyond my wildest imagination. When I discovered my Why It Matters was 'to figure it out,' all the pieces to my life's puzzle began to fall into place. Since I was a small child, my goal was to figure 'it' out: toys, games, conversations, situations, relationships. You name it, and I am trying to figure it out.

When I can't figure things out, I become frustrated and stressed. I am not able to let go of the 'it.' This has kept me stuck and unproductive at times. Now that I have discovered this about myself, I can release the notion that I have to figure everything out. At work, I have been able to delegate assignments to folks who have the knowledge, skills, and abilities to figure out things when I am stuck. I am asking for help for the first time in my life. It has been life changing and has improved my productivity at work as well as my relationships with others. Ask my wife!

NAME: SUSANNA
OCCUPATION: ACADEMIA
AGE: 63
LOCATION: SONORA, MEXICO
WHY IT MATTERS: TO SAVE

It is funny to look back over the course of your life after discovering your Why It Matters. You can see how it has shown up in a positive way. You also see how it has shown up in a negative way. My Why It Matters is 'to save.' Looking back, bullying was my biggest concern during my school life. I took it upon myself to be the enforcer and protector of all children being bullied.

Today, in the workforce, I try to save people at work, too. I notice that during meetings, when someone is having difficulty expressing their thoughts, I quickly jump in to save them by saying something like, "I think Joe is trying to say is…." I have learned that I am not 'saving' at all. I am actually doing the opposite. I am robbing someone of a growth opportunity.

Now that I have discovered my Why It Matters, I can stop myself and think about what to do. Keeping my Why It Matters in check has strengthened my relationships with my team. Just the other day, one of my teammates stopped me and thanked me for not interrupting when he talked at the meeting. Wow!

In everything I do, I want to make sure I am adding value. Growing up, this looked a lot like adding my 'two cents' to every conversation. This has been with me throughout my entire life.

At work, I always contribute to conversations during meetings. I have to keep my Why It Matters in check because sometimes I talk just to talk. If I am not sharing my thoughts or opinions, I don't feel like a contributor.

I have learned that, after discovering my Why It Matters, during certain situations, silence might be the best value I can add. I have never thought of silence as adding value, but it does. My colleagues are opening up, and I am fully present by listening to what others have to say. Instead of making statements, I have been able to ask more questions to better engage in two-way conversations. My wife sees it at home too, which is an added bonus.

NAME: ADAM
OCCUPATION: ACCOUNTANT
AGE: 26
LOCATION: OREGON, USA
WHY IT MATTERS: TO DO IT MY WAY

I like to do things my way. Even as a child, I would argue with my mother about getting dressed. She would offer her opinion about what I should wear. I did not listen. From a young age of five, I wanted to do it my way. I chose what I was going to wear to school. As a young adult, I was convinced that I operated best when doing things my way.

The process of uncovering my Why It Matters has been a journey of self-reflection. While uncomfortable at times, taking the time to step back and learn more about what motivates me has been, and continues to be, a meaningful experience.

Understanding myself a little better, both what drives me and what holds me back, has given me the gift of insight when approaching new and challenging situations. I am slowly learning that I can't always do things my own way, and I probably shouldn't. I set aside my pride and ego to listen to others and their ideas.

NAME: GREG
OCCUPATION: VICE PRESIDENT OF MARKETING
AGE: 68
LOCATION: ONTARIO, CANADA
WHY IT MATTERS: TO BE IN IT

Being 'in it,' for me, means that I am involved in everything. I have to be invited to meetings. I want the 'scoop,' the latest information. I need to be kept abreast of everything that's going on. People have to let me know what they are doing. Some people think this is tiring… or suffocating.

Well, I discovered my Why It Matters three years ago. Since then, my life has completely turned around. I am very aware that I can be 'in it' way too much. Now, I have a checklist. Before I decide to be 'in it,' I ask myself a series of questions: "Is it important?" "Is it worthy of my time?" "How long will this take without me in it? With me in it?", and "Do I need to bother?" and "Will it matter in a month, a quarter, or a year?" The answers are clear, and I always listen to them.

I have to tell you, it took time for this checklist to become a habit. I had to learn to trust my own system. Then the craziest thing happened. I thought, "If I can create a habit at work, I should be able to do it in my home life." So I made a checklist for my diet and my weight. In two years, I lost over 80 pounds. I have even run two marathons.

You never know, until you start reflecting, how much you can do and how many important things you can change. Knowing Why It Matters, I am now able to understand myself.

NAME: RUPAL
OCCUPATION: PHYSICIAN
AGE: 43
LOCATION: NEW SOUTH WALES, AUSTRALIA
WHY IT MATTERS: TO BE THE BEST

The term "awareness" was the backbone of my experience as the student of a Sherpa Coach. After initial exploration and then identification of my Why It Matters, I was able to see how so many of my actions in the different realms of my life (work, home, community) were actually motivated by the SAME Why It Matters. It has allowed me to understand WHY I do what I do (or don't do) and to understand times where my Why It Matters paralyzed me or caused me to behave in an ineffective way.

I was able to alter my behavior by stopping and reflecting on my motives. Since my Why It Matters is "being the best," the knowledge of it allows me to pursue that, or allows me to actively choose not to pursue it. To be the best is exhausting and has cost me time, relationships, and my own sanity. It has also gotten me to where I am today. I am now able to push the 'pause' button to see if and when I need to be the best and what the benefits and costs will be. I am able to make the conscious choice to act in the most effective manner and sustain that effective behavior.

NAME: MIKE
OCCUPATION: SYSTEM ANALYST
AGE: 57
LOCATION: NORTH CAROLINA, USA
WHY IT MATTERS: TO ADVOCATE

I was raised to do things right and to be fair. When I realized that my Why It Matters is "to advocate," I felt relieved that my value system aligned with my passion to be a campaigner for what is right and fair. In fact, it was reassuring that I could be "right," and then it was alarming that I could also be "wrong" at the same time. Of course, that was when my Why It Matters went off the charts!

It was hard to look at myself and admit that my true weakness was the opposite of my Why It Matters. I'm a strong believer in social justice. Advocating for what's right and fair fits with who I am. What I realized, however, is that when I feel undervalued, ignored, or overlooked, I get angry. My outbursts and cursing on the job created an unbearable environment, I was placed on probation. What? I just was trying to make things right and fair by advocating.

Oh, I still have this value. It will always be my Why It Matters. I just have learned to be less aggressive when I am advocating for righteousness and fairness. I'm using my Sherpa tools to be more deliberate in my interactions with coworkers. I was also surprised to see how my relationship with my wife improved. I guess I was an angry person and didn't realize the impact of my words and actions at work and at home.

Some say I'm a whole new person! I'm still the same Mike. I just have learned how to deal and advocate for what I think is right at appropriate times.

NAME: IVY
OCCUPATION: HR GENERALIST
AGE: 42
LOCATION: MARYLAND, USA
WHY IT MATTERS: TO BE VALUED FOR MY KNOWLEDGE

I have worked in Human Resources my entire career. I am the "go to" person, and I like being that person. However, it really ticks me off when I'm questioned. There's a right way and a wrong way, and that's my job to figure out. I'm the expert, aren't I?

Wow! That describes my Why It Matters and my weakness! While I know a lot about HR, I was taking things personally. I thought I was being criticized, instead of seeing that a question is simply a question. I cut people off, snapped at them, and generally made people afraid to approach me.

Yeah, I was right and knowledgeable, and everyone was going to know it! When I started to use the QTIP, a reminder to Quit Taking It Personally, and the Three-Sentence Rule, I relaxed in my responses to others. To my surprise, people came to me more often for my input because of my expertise. It's shocking how a little change in my behavior gave me more of what I wanted: to be valued for my knowledge.

NAME: GARY
OCCUPATION: INDUSTRIAL DESIGNER
AGE: 35
LOCATION: ABU DHABI, DUBAI
WHY IT MATTERS: TO ENGINEER

I just like to make sure everything goes smoothly. But here is the caveat- I make sure it is equal, balanced, organized, and impeccable as well. Things need to be built, designed, and manufactured the way I envision them. If it is not engineered that way, I simply break down and can't function. Needless to say, life is NOT like that. Nothing is ever in a straight row.

Discovering my Why It Matters took time, but when I found it, everything I have ever done in my life started to make sense, from building Lego forts as a 6 year old to the way I ask my wife to organize my ties. I now know that it is a fundamental issue for me when it goes overboard. So I keep it in check, all the time. It takes work, but it is worth the effort.

NAME: ANDY
OCCUPATION: CEO
AGE: 60
LOCATION: GREATER LONDON, UK
WHY IT MATTERS: TO BE HEARD

I have been an executive for 25 years. I started as a VP of a small company. I know how to do my job, and do it well. I can't be in a meeting without being heard. I can't be on a conference call without being heard. I can't be at the dining room table without being heard. So many times, I am able to speak up and really solve some major issues. Unfortunately I have spoken out too many times, both at home and at work. I have micromanaged my family and my employees. I have made sure they heard me, and heard me well. Now, they can't even think for themselves.

NAME: MELANIE
OCCUPATION: VP HEALTH CARE
AGE: 54
LOCATION: VIRGINIA, USA
WHY IT MATTERS: TO BE GOOD ENOUGH

It's not exaggeration when Sherpa coaches tell you that discovering your Why It Matters is a powerful exercise. It is both humbling and undeniably true to the core. I wanted my Why It Matters to be "to make an impact." That sounds really important doesn't it? But when we started to discuss how our ingrained messages shape our Why It Matters, the image of me pedaling a tricycle behind my sister who was on a bicycle (and who is 13 months older than me) overwhelmed me. I remember thinking, "I have to prove I'm good enough." It didn't matter that in reality she had the advantage of age, physical ability, and a better bike. I then recognized all the ways I expend energy and create stress for myself trying to be "good enough" at work. Interestingly, "good enough" is also my strength.

I am not a perfectionist. I have made a successful career by creating start-ups in healthcare where "good enough to go" has been my mantra. What I do now is ask myself: "Who defines 'good enough' in this situation? Me or someone else? Is it reasonable? If not, how can I define 'good enough' in a way that is easy on me and valuable to the organization?" I now have a sign hanging above my desk that says "define good enough." It helps me take a more realistic look at requests at work. And that's good enough for me.

NAME: ANTHONY
OCCUPATION: HEALTH ADMINISTRATOR
AGE: 32
LOCATION: CALIFORNIA, USA
WHY IT MATTERS: TO BE WANTED

My Why It Matters is "to be wanted." Knowing my Why It Matters and its relevance in my business life, I can see how this affects my relationships with people. I am aware it is unrealistic to expect others to always want my services or want me around. I no longer take it personally when someone is not responsive to a connection.

I know I need to be wanted, but I do not let this need color how others respond to me. I realize that many of my behaviors are driven by my Why It Matters. Without this knowledge, I would waste a lot of time and energy reacting to other people just being themselves. I am not the center of their universe, and knowing that has made me free.

NAME: RUTH
OCCUPATION: ACADEMIC/PROFESSOR
AGE: 60
LOCATION: GEORGIA, USA
WHY IT MATTERS: TO BELONG

Discovering my Why It Matters has been very freeing for me. I have often fought against my desire to be in the center of things, or to be part of the crowd. I didn't realize that 'belonging' is at my core. It is who I am. My nature to be sharing and giving, to be the gift-giver instead of the recipient, is all part of wanting to belong.

What I can do now is play to my Why It Matters. I can take the initiative and feel completely comfortable working hard "to belong." If I want to be part of a particular group, my motivation will be directed toward making that happen!

One of my weaknesses is giving people an answer they should discover for themselves. I have to be the one to know things. Someone asked, "What would happen if you didn't know?" Panic set in. The room started spinning. My eyes welled up. It hit me. I had found my Why It Matters. I remembered, as a 17-year-old girl, having a "chat" with my parents. They told me things I had never heard. I walked away from the chat thinking, "This will never happen to me again." Ever since then, I avoid situations like that.

To know is my Why It Matters, and knowing is, without a doubt, what drives me to my core. My position in Human Resources provides me the perfect platform to observe the organization and people, ask questions, and go from 'big picture' to detail seamlessly.

Sharing my Why It Matters has helped my family and coworkers to understand that I have a huge need for information. I am inquisitive. It's made me a stronger individual by being able to connect all the pieces related to my strengths, weaknesses, and values to my need for information, observation, and inquiry and, therefore, to my need to know.

Discovering that "to know" is what drives me answered the question of "What would happen if you didn't know?" It finally gave me the freedom to allow others to do their own work and, in the process, be able to find the answer for themselves. It relieved me from the burden of having to know.

NAME: E.J.
OCCUPATION: DIRECTOR, TALENT DEVELOPMENT
AGE: 40
LOCATION: CIUDAD REAL, SPAIN
WHY IT MATTERS: TO BE UNDERSTOOD

I am fortunate to work with a colleague who has gone through the Sherpa certification, so I had advance warning that discovering my Why It Matters would be an arduous process. I was ready for the hard work, yet not prepared for the emotional rollercoaster and soul-searching involved in the discovery process. The word "discovery" may be misleading - it suggests one might stumble upon their Why It Matters. They won't! It's more like capturing a big-game animal or an elusive fugitive.

No pressure here, you're simply trying to identify one short phrase that gets to the true core of who you are and explains everything you've ever done. As you might imagine, there are many forces at play here, not the least of which is the ego. The temptation to search for a noble sounding Why It Matters is a strong one. It can take some time to get past the intoxicating effects of a Why It Matters such as "to make the world a better place," or "to benefit mankind," and get to the true, unvarnished essence of who you are and what makes you tick.

But finding your Why It Matters is worth all the effort. The feeling you get when you finally hit it right on the head is so powerful and emotional; it is overwhelming. The moment I realized my Why It Matters is "to be understood," everything made sense - from raising my hand every five minutes in first grade, to participating in drama and music in High School, to teaching college, to writing, recording, and performing music, to designing and facilitating leadership programs, to choosing my wife and the way we raise our kids, - it all makes sense now!

Even writing this paragraph is driven by a desire to be understood. Everything I have ever done, every big decision I have ever made and all the people I have chosen in my life can be explained by my Why It Matters. With this new understanding, I believe I am perfectly prepared to chart the next chapters in my life, both personally and professionally. Put another way, because of my Why It Matters, I know who I am. I know why I do what I do. I know what I need to be: motivated, engaged, and successful. As my 6-year-old daughter Alex would say, "Daddy, that ROCKS!"

NAME: PAM
OCCUPATION: SOCIAL WORKER
AGE: 55
LOCATION: ALBERTA, CANADA
WHY IT MATTERS: TO BE NEEDED

I lived through a number of 'seasons' before I realized my Why It Matters. A couple of Sherpa friends assisted me along the journey of discovering. One fall afternoon, I got in my car with my dog and a pen and paper. I drove on the road alongside a river until I found a unique tree where I could sit and reflect.

And that I did. I wrote and wrote. I felt the cool breeze and rustling leaves as if they were an inspiration to my words. Every word I wrote to the following questions followed a theme throughout my life. What motivates me? What has followed me all my life? What did my parents teach me? What is important to me?

I am a caring person. My life encircles helping. Most of the time, that works out just fine. But when the essence of my Why It Matters runs amok, I am a pain in someone's side! Surely, someone needs my help!

Learning my Why It Matters has been life-changing for me. And for that, I am forever grateful.

NAME: XENA
OCCUPATION: VP SALES
AGE: 37
LOCATION: FLORIDA, USA
WHY IT MATTERS: TO BE VALUED

So many of us are on 'automatic pilot' in our daily lives that we do not take time to find out why we repeat our mistakes. That's just crazy. You know you'll do it again, and the cycle will drive you nuts. Well, it takes time to find out your one key motivating factor - your Why It Matters. And you can get help to ensure you get it right. That's what I did, and it made a huge difference.

I thought I had it: "To add value." My Sherpa Coach said, "No, that's not it." I was shocked. Not surprised, literally shocked. How could anyone know my personal Why It Matters? Because they see it more than I do! I'm not observing myself, but others are observing me.

With prompting from my coach, I reflected on what I gain out of doing things for others, hence, "to be valued." It's why I work so hard on stuff I don't need to be involved in: to be valued for my efforts. It was time to let that go.

I learned to let others grow, and I do not take on unnecessary things. I focus on the strategic rather than the tactical. I have taken a ton of weight off my shoulders, and that is clearly worth the time I invested in myself.

NAME: K.J.
OCCUPATION: CIVIL SERVICE
AGE: 40
LOCATION: BRITISH COLUMBIA, CANADA
WHY IT MATTERS: TO DEFEND

Discovering my Why It Matters has allowed me to identify when my behavior is not appreciated. My Why It Matters is 'to defend.' Before discovering my Why It Matters, I was constantly involved in situations where I did not belong. For example, my 8-year-old daughter and an older nephew had a disagreement. I found myself jumping in, "defending" my daughter. When it was all said and done, my daughter said, "Mom, I do not need your help."

Defensiveness drives me to get involved when I am not needed. As the oldest sibling of three, I was always in a position to defend myself and my younger sister and brother. In turn, I needed to defend anyone who was being taken advantage of. Knowing this has allowed me to simplify my life and diminish my load of responsibilities.

NAME: AARON
OCCUPATION: PRESIDENT, ENERGY SERVICES
AGE: 54
LOCATION: CONNECTICUT, USA
WHY IT MATTERS: TO BE THE GO TO

The 'go to' person can be turned to for knowledge, advice, or reliable results in a crucial situation: The journey to fully discovering my Why It Matters has been a satisfying one. Once I could grasp my strengths and weaknesses and determine my Why It Matters, I maintained more control over my behaviors by knowing how situations, words, phrases, certain people, or certain relationships could bring out the best... and the worst in me.

With a Why It Matters of 'to be the go to,' I quickly understood why I, at times, felt the need to stretch myself too thin or hold myself to extremely high standards.

As I began to better understand where my behaviors were coming from, I found that I could channel them to a more positive energy and prevent myself from becoming overwhelmed or controlled by my weaknesses. I see my choices more clearly, and I am reaching a higher potential of becoming the best 'me' I can be. Through this process, I have seen significant gains in my self-confidence and look forward to continued growth and development.

THE AUTHORS

BRENDA CORBETT

Brenda Corbett developed the concept of 'Why It Matters' as she created the Sherpa process for executive coaching. Why It Matters is an important part of her university textbook: "The Sherpa Guide: Process-Driven Executive Coaching". This book has been the foundation for certification programs at ten major universities. Corbett's later works include: "BE... Don't Do: The Sherpa Guide to Coaching for Managers" (2009) and "Impact on Business: The Sherpa Guide to Business, Behavior and You" (2012).

A native of Canada, Corbett lives in Cincinnati, Ohio in the USA and maintains a strong business presence in South Africa. Brenda Corbett's ideas have changed individuals and organizations, including leadership teams at Toyota, L'Oreal, Duke Energy and Stanley Black & Decker. As an educator, Corbett is spearheading development of the Sherpa Leadership Institute, and online vehicle for leadership development and executive coach training.

JENNIFER CHLOUPEK

With "Why It Matters", Jennifer Chloupek makes a strong debut as a business writer. Chloupek has over 15 years of experience as an educator, strategic planner, and leader in the public sector. She is a certified Sherpa Executive Coach and experienced facilitator and trainer. Jenn is a Workforce Development Specialist at the National Cancer Institute. She received her Master's Degree in Education from Towson University and has served as adjunct faculty for the University.

SHERPA COACHING

Sherpa Coaching, co-founded by Brenda Corbett, is best known for the Sherpa process for executive coaching. The Sherpa process is consistently ranked as the most widely used coaching process in the world. Other offerings from Sherpa Coaching include the longest-running event for coaches, and the Executive Coaching Survey, annual market research started in 2005. For more information, visit: www.sherpacoaching.com.

As "Why It Matters" goes to press, Corbett is working on her next book, "Selfware: The Marriage of Executive Coaching and Neuroscience" in collaboration with Prof. Justin Kennedy, a leader in neuroscience research at the University of Pretoria in South Africa and Dean at the Monarch Business School in Switzerland.